Harry Greene is a recognized expert in the field of
DIY and home improvement and is well known to
millions of viewers as present
series *On the House* and *Baza*
consultant to B&Q Superstore
he draws on years of experie
demonstrate DIY problems a
Harry also lectures and preser
confere
article
He is married with three children and lives in
London.

# HARRY GREENE

# D·I·Y

# PROBLEM

# SOLVER

**A PAN ORIGINAL**
**PAN BOOKS**
LONDON, SYDNEY AND AUCKLAND

First published 1990 by Pan Books Ltd,
Cavaye Place, London SW10 9PG

9 8 7 6 5 4 3 2 1

ISBN 0 330 31168 9 paperback
ISBN 0 330 31952 3 hardback

Photoset by Parker Typesetting Service, Leicester
Printed and bound in Great Britain by
Clays Ltd, St Ives plc

# CONTENTS

If we make one major investment in our lives it's buying a home. In fact, nearly 70 per cent of the houses in this country are now owner occupied. Whether you live in a small terraced house or a detached house, recurring problems of repair and maintenance are common in all parts of the country. Each year in towns and cities all over the country I advise and demonstrate DIY techniques and building principles. This provides a unique opportunity for me to learn at first hand what problems are confronting people in their homes. Rotten floors, condensation problems, knocking in pipes and blistering paintwork are, in the minds of most people, specialist jobs for the tradesman. This of course is not so. All you need are step-by-step instructions, common sense, basic tools and limited expertise to be able to carry out all these repair jobs and more.

Often the DIYer is enthusiastic but unaware of the need for planning or unsure of the correct way of tackling a job. Once the initial planning stage is over and the preparation work complete, you'll be amazed to find that you're more than half-way there. This will provide the impetus to get on with the next job. You will feel happier because your home will look better, it will certainly have a longer life and will improve in value.

For over thirty years I have been pioneering DIY in this country, in books, newspapers, magazines and on radio and television. During the three-year run of BBC2's DIY programme *On the House* we received over 250,000 letters. People were fascinated to see ordinary viewers in their own homes solving a repair or renovation job under my guidance. This item, called Troubleshooting, has stirred the imagination not only of viewers but of manufacturers too. The DIY industry is booming. Manufacturers are becoming more sensitive to the needs of the DIY consumer. The philosophy of designers appears to be to maximize both use and value by developing well-designed DIY products which are easy to use and readily affordable. Manufacturers' and designers' up-to-date approaches to traditional problems have led to many unique and innovative solutions. Screwing down a replacement floor with a conventional screwdriver might take half a day, but by using a rechargeable cordless power screwdriver it will take a quarter of the time! Scrubbing a patio with grease spots and mould growth could take half a day if done by hand, but hire a new high-powered water jet and you'll be ready for a well-deserved drink after an hour's work.

I often find people panicky when confronted with the simplest repair problem. But, of course, it's the lack of knowledge of tools, materials and procedures that is the prime cause for concern. Read on! I hope to inspire you to dig out and replace rotting floor joists, to stop soot stains spoiling your decorations and to stop those sneaky cold draughts around the house. I hope that this guide to the trouble spots around your home will become *your* DIY problem solver.

# CHAPTER ONE

# TOOLS
# AND
# EQUIPMENT

A basic tool kit is all that is necessary for whatever DIY problem you have to solve. Don't ever be put off by thinking that you have to stock up with a comprehensive assortment of different tools for each job. Lots of DIY jobs can be solved over a weekend, in which case it is very easy to hire expensive tools that you might not have or even want to buy. This means that you can choose exactly the right specialist tools to suit the job.

The tools that you collect should be the best that you can afford, so stick to the tried and tested brands. If you have a dry shed, basement, workshop or garage then find space on a wall to put up a tool board. Each tool can be supported by a hook or two nails. Once the tool is in position draw around it with a felt pen and print a note on the board to remind everyone to return the tool to its proper place after it is finished with. Each tool should be used only for the purpose for which it was designed! For example, never use a claw hammer for chipping at concrete and never use a screwdriver for levering lids off paint tins. Learn all you can about sharpening tools and keeping handles and moving parts in good repair. All tools and accessories come with an illustrated leaflet; keep all instructions so that you learn how to use and maintain each of the tools properly. The cutting edges of planes and chisels are easily maintained with a double-sided oil stone and an inexpensive honing guide. Always keep a slightly oiled rag in a plastic container so that you can wipe over all steel tools. This will help prevent rust attacking them. Don't forget that the precious part of a screwdriver is the end or tip of the blade. This is designed only for driving or removing screws, and not for prying up nail heads, chipping away cement or punching nails.

Most homes possess an electric drill. It is my first choice in putting together a basic tool kit; add to this a claw hammer, a panel saw, a tenon saw, a steel tape, a junior hacksaw, a pump screwdriver with interchangeable blades, a No. 2 cross-head screwdriver, an electrical test screwdriver, pincers, insulated-handle pliers, a bradawl, a couple of bevelled-edged chisels, a multi-purpose trimming tool, a trimming knife with a retractable blade and a staple gun. Two other essentials to make up the complete basic kit are a short aluminium stepladder and a portable workbench.

After successfully solving one DIY problem, there is less anxiety and worry about the next project! Maybe it's a job involving punching nails in below the surface of wood or cutting decorative curves in timber, so a nail punch or a coping saw finds itself on a list for your birthday or Christmas present! As you gain expertise and become more proficient, you will find it much easier to tackle the next repair or maintenance job. You'll add a full-sized hacksaw to your tool kit, an adjustable wrench, a couple of chisels including a mortice chisel, a smoothing plane, a hand drill, a carpenter's tri-square, a general-purpose flat file, a spirit level, and a set of electric drill bits and masonry bits in separate plastic cases.

Professionals use the best brushes, rollers and pads available. A good-quality brush bearing a respected brand name will ensure that you get a professional finish to your paintwork. The difference between good and bad brushes lies in the length of the bristles and the compact but springy nature of the natural hog's-hair bristles. If you break off in the middle of a painting job make sure that you have a wrap-around container for the brush, with a specially formulated liquid to keep it moist, even overnight. Castle products have produced a number of aids of this nature for the DIY enthusiast.

Keep the instructions on the side of a tin of paint clear of dripping paint. You'll always need to check the appropriate solvent for cleaning brushes at the end of the day. To clean a brush thoroughly, press out as much of the residual paint as you can on

to a newspaper with a flat piece of wood or the back of a knife. After washing it in whatever solvent the makers recommend, clean it thoroughly in warm water and detergent, followed by a rinse in hot clean water. Never stand a brush on the bristles to dry, but let it hang. A hole drilled into the wooden handle is the easiest way of supporting it.

Rollers are the best tools for painting walls and ceilings. Some rollers have a fixed sleeve but most popular are those with interchangeable sleeves. Lamb's-wool is a good general-purpose material for use with vinyl matt emulsion and on textured surfaces. Another is a short-pile mohair sleeve used mostly with eggshell, vinyl silk or solid emulsion paint. Cheaper foam sleeves are really not worth buying because they tend to spray and spatter the paint. When you buy a roller, the instructions on the packaging will be very explicit regarding cleaning and maintaining. As with brushes, remove all residual paint from the roller by using the correct solvent, wash thoroughly in warm water and detergent, then rinse thoroughly in hot water. Roll out as much moisture as possible on newspaper before hanging up to dry.

Paint pads will never compete with the traditional method of applying paint with a brush! However, as they are easy to manipulate and can cover large surfaces very quickly the DIY beginner might find them useful. Some pads are easier to handle because they are hinged, thus enabling them to get around obstacles. Use paint pads with a paint tray but clean and maintain the paint pad as with a roller and don't forget the paint tray has to be cleaned too!

# SAFETY FIRST!

Manufacturers are constantly upgrading and improving safety standards in materials and tools. Previously a number of wall coatings contained asbestos, some cleaning fluids contained harmful compounds and some tools were positively dangerous. Happily, more stringent rules and regulations now cover the manufacture of harmful products and potentially dangerous tools; if you learn and follow the safety measures listed below, you will avoid the risk of a serious accident.

Remember: the best DIYer is as much aware of safety as the need to solve a DIY problem successfully!

## ELECTRICITY

Write these few notes on a label and stick it near your consumer unit:

1  Always turn off at the mains, and isolate any circuit that you may be working on by removing the relevant fuse.

2  Never work on a circuit with the current still turned on.

3  If the fuse carrier is removable keep it with you until you're ready to restore the supply.

4  Dry your hands thoroughly before touching plugs and sockets.

5  Before working on any electrical appliance take the plug from the socket.

6  Ensure that the correctly rated fuse is used in a plug. This should be 3-amp up to 720 watts and 13-amp up to 3000 watts.

7  Use the correct fuse rating in fuse carriers covering the circuits. The lighting circuit needs a 5-amp fuse; a storage heater needs a 20-amp fuse; the ring main circuit (power) needs a 30-amp fuse; a shower unit needs a 30-amp fuse; a cooker up to 12kW needs a 30-amp fuse, over 12kW a 45-amp fuse.

## DANGEROUS LIQUIDS

1  Wood preservatives these days are very attractive; most are harmless to plants when dry and have long-lasting protective qualities. However, most of them are flammable, so take extra precautions when using them. Remember: no smoking and certainly no naked lights. Wear gloves and protective clothing, and use a face mask in constricted areas.

2  If ever you have to use acid, for example to clean old quarry tiles, wear p.v.c. gloves, protective clothing and goggles. When mixing with water, always add acid to water, never the other way round. Mark all containers clearly, and keep them out of the way of children and animals.

3  Most chemical paint strippers are harmful if splashed on to the skin or into the eyes, so take extra precautions when working with them. Jelly stripper is based on methylene chloride, and thick paste stripper is caustic based, so both need to be used very carefully. Vinyl

work gloves and safety goggles are essential, as is a face mask and good ventilation. If you follow the manufac- turer's instructions you, your children and your pets should come to no harm.

## POWER TOOLS

Power tools are strong, sturdy and safe pro- vided that you read and follow the manufac- turer's instructions exactly.

1   Always use a properly insulated purpose-made extension lead.
2   Sometimes it's tempting to lift a power tool by its flex. Don't!
3   Remember always to remove the chuck key before using a power drill. Never wear loose clothing when using a power drill. If you have to change a drill bit or an attachment don't forget to unplug the drill first.
4   When fitting a new blade to a circular saw, the teeth at the bottom of the blade must face in the direction of the cut.
5   Never use a saw without the blade guard in place.
6   Never allow the cable of a power tool to snake in on the work.

## OTHER HAZARDS

1   When chipping at bricks, stone or con- crete with a chisel, wear inexpensive plastic goggles to protect your eyes. You might even use a DIY angle-grinder for cutting slabs or bricks, in which case wear a gauze face mask, so that you don't breathe in harmful dust.
2   Glass is very easy to handle and cut if you take the correct precautions. Always carry glass on its edge (protec- ted with pads of folded paper or card- board) by gripping the top and bottom edges; it's safer, of course, to wear pro- tective gloves. When hacking out broken glass from a frame, wear strong canvas gloves and goggles.
3   Lightweight aluminium ladders are strong and safe provided that they are used wisely and properly. Carry a ladder upright and erect it safely before you use it. Never lean to the side, always move the ladder if the work is out of reach. Ensure that the base of the ladder is on firm ground, and anchor it top and bottom. Stepladders topple if used sideways.

# CHAPTER TWO

# OUTSIDE

# YOUR

# HOME

## PROBLEMS WITH TREES

Trees can soften the harsh lines of unattractive buildings or complement the beauty of classical architecture. As part of soft landscaping they are essential to create a more gentle environment in towns and inner cities.

Mature trees close to our homes can become part of our lives. However, these 'friends' close to our homes, either on our property or in the street outside, can cause trouble. If you intend planting a tree close to your house, think very carefully about the species and the proximity to your property. The structure of the house can be seriously damaged by a maturing tree close by. To offset any potential damage from tree roots, plan your landscaping so that a tree is planted with a distance of greater than half the mature height of the tree between it and your property. Some trees spread their roots further than the mature height of the tree; check with your supplier before you purchase.

If tree roots are a problem already, seek the advice of your local Planning Department. You cannot cut down or lop a tree on your property without Planning Permission

if you live in a conservation area, or if a tree on your property is registered as 'protected'. Although the tree may be causing problems, you could be prosecuted for felling it without obtaining the necessary permission. However it is possible to lop and prune branches and to sever some of the roots to prevent further damage. Your local nursery-garden adviser will be pleased to tell you what to do.

There are a number of ways in which roots can damage the drainage system around your property and the ground below it. Roots grow and spread as they seek food and moisture and are no respectors of obstacles. Large roots are very strong and can break rigid earthenware drainage pipes. Manholes, drain runs and collared joints can be damaged or become totally blocked, so it is essential to monitor as far as possible the condition of all your house drainage system.

The breakdown of your drainage system due to root movement is serious enough, but not as serious as the potential damage to foundations and the actual structure of the house. The first part of a house to be built is the foundation. This is built on a

Trees that cause most problems to buildings are: Poplar (*See illustration opposite*) **1**. Ash **2**. Oak **3**. Weeping Willow **4**. Plane **5**. Elm. Slightly less serious are: **6**. Silver Birch **7**. Maple **8**. Beech **9**. Lawson Cypress.

A part sectional illustration to show the serious consequences of planting a poplar tree too close to a house. The soil can dry out and the roots spread, searching for moisture from under the foundations, causing the earth to collapse and foundations to slip. Cracks then appear from windows to the edge of a building and to the ground.

compacted or solid soil base. The whole structure of the building is then keyed together and stabilized. Any weakening of that subsoil supporting the structure will cause movement, creating structural faults and cracks. Trees can do this in two ways.

A mature tree is a thirsty tree and it searches for moisture through its roots. When those roots remove too much moisture from beneath the foundation the earth collapses, resulting in subsidence. Cracks appearing in the corner of a building to or from a window or door opening where the structure is weakest, is often a sign that this movement is occurring.

To offset the possibility of this type of problem, make a full check of your drainage system by rodding all the drains using a set of hired drain rods, and checking on the structure of gulleys and manholes. Look for any sign of cracking in the walls closest to a mature tree. Tree roots can be trimmed without affecting the growth of the tree but do seek the advice of a tree surgeon. If serious structural damage is suspected, ask your local Building Control Officer to visit you by appointment; he will confirm whether or not underpinning is necessary. This process involves excavating below the original foundation in the problem area and pouring concrete in to provide extra strength and stability.

Conversely, structural damage can be caused to a property when a mature tree close to it is cut down. Damage is then caused by heave as opposed to subsidence. Over the years soil and subsoil become stabilized and a tree taking moisture through its roots from this ground can help to stabilize the surrounding ground. If the tree is cut down the ground is suddenly left with a great deal of moisture and actually swells as more is added to it. This causes upward movement of the ground which can

then distort the corner of a building, causing cracks in exterior walls and displacement inside.

The problem of heave can be overcome very simply by laying land drains. Ask your Local Building Control Officer for advice on laying land drains. Channels are dug at a certain depth running to a soak-away, and land drains are laid surrounded by pea gravel. The soak-away is a square hole filled with rubble. Depth of drains and size of soak-away depend entirely upon local conditions.

Clematis, honeysuckle and ivy may also give problems in the long term. Tiles and slates can be disturbed and pushed out of position by strong ivy growth, resulting in water penetration and damage to the interior fabric of the house. More commonly, the surface-water drainage system is affected by these climbers; the smaller bore-pipe can easily be blocked once a root starts to penetrate it.

These plants need not necessarily affect or damage the walls of your property, though. They send out suckers only to hold the plant in place. Position them where they cannot do any root damage to the pipes and gulleys that take water from gutters and surface drainage and, with careful pruning and training, problems above ground can be offset.

## PROTECTING EXTERIOR WOOD

Wherever you live, be it town, countryside or seaside, protecting the exterior of your home can present problems. Every exterior surface is subject to the blistering heat of the sun which distorts paint and wood; to frost

and ice which can split open timber joints and even masonry; and to gales which drive rain-water into the fabric of the house, causing rot. Add to this sulphur, salts, pollutants and you begin to see how the outside of the home deserves more attention and protection than it probably gets!

In many cases something more than ordinary stain or gloss is required. High-quality coatings are now available formulated for specific uses, providing the solution to every DIYer's particular sealing, staining and protecting problem.

For years the building industry has enjoyed the benefits of pre-treated timber and now manufacturers and timber merchants are much more aware of the needs of the DIY consumer and home improver. Prefabricated sheds, garages, fencing units and garden furniture are manufactured to higher standards and the timber is pre-treated with preservative which carries a ten-year guarantee. Unfortunately, much of the timber around the outsides of our homes – in doors, window frames, decorative boards, cladding, wooden steps and balconies, gates and fencing, and much more – suffers the consequences of not having been treated. Manufacturers have invested a great deal in research, developing stains, varnishes, preservatives, primers and unique, durable top-coatings which prevent moisture penetration and resist ultraviolet rays from the sun. Additionally these top-coatings allow wood to shrink and stretch, providing a lasting, protective surface which is resistant to cracking, peeling or flaking.

There are products to suit different timber finishes. Exterior woodwork also comes under attack from weather pollutants and fungus. However, it can be protected by applying a durable product that is formulated to protect exterior timber for up to ten years.

### Rot

Problems of rot in wood or attack by woodworm have to be tackled immediately. Woodworm is the commonly used generic term for a number of species of wood-boring insects. Eggs are laid in or on timber and the larvae feed upon and bore through the wood leaving a network of holes which can weaken the structure. Remove and burn any timber that is obviously past repair. Replace with pre-treated matching timber. (*See below.*) Dry rot is usually associated with damp conditions in darkened interiors. Timber attacked by wet rot, which is a less serious condition, must also be removed and replaced. Once the damp condition is removed and the source of the problem solved there should be no further attacks of wet rot. There are proprietary brands of preservative available to treat the surrounding timbers.

## PREPARING AND PRESERVING TIMBER

With all DIY jobs, preparation is perhaps as important as any part of the job, and most timber problems outside the home are the result of poor preparation and poor protection. Never paint or seal damp timber. We are used to the traditional three-coat system of painting on new exterior timber by which we decorate and protect the timber in one. This system of painting provides an impervious barrier to rain-water penetration. Unfortunately, it also traps any moisture or resins in the timber. Blisters appearing on window frames or outside doors are a direct result of poor preparation. Moisture or resin is being drawn out of the timber but has nowhere to go. The result is that the film of paint loses its adhesion and is pushed into a blister.

### Treating new pre-made timbers

Fitting a new front door, or even an up-and-over garage door, is not beyond the scope of a competent DIYer. The timber doors arrive in a plastic covering ready for whatever colour and treatment you wish to apply. Whether the new timber you are about to protect and seal is for a new front door, garage doors, new gate posts and gate, window frames or perhaps a new timber conservatory, be certain to use the new microporous sealing system, which will allow moisture in the wood to escape in a controlled way, but prevent water penetration. Always order any timber product that you intend to seal or paint at least a week before you intend to fit it. Remove any plastic covering and allow the product to lie flat, with space for movement of air, so that it can acclimatize to indoor humidity. This will ensure that the wood is sufficiently dry to paint or seal.

With all painting techniques, good preparation is most important. Give all surfaces a rub down with fine glass paper, always sanding in the direction of the grain. One of the enemies of paint is damp, the other dust, so be certain to remove all traces of sanding with a clean cloth dampened with white spirit.

There is a range of colours to choose from and the modern microporous stains are suitable as a long-lasting exterior wood treatment whether you are dealing with softwood or hardwood. Paints and stains in this range produce a film that contains microscopically small pores, which allow the moisture in the wood to breathe out naturally as water vapour. This means that vapour pressure does not build up beneath the paint film. When temperatures rise, the wood treatment remains flexible and expands and contracts with the natural movement of the timber. The build-up of the impervious film on the surface of the timber makes it ideal for painting windows and other exterior woodwork where moisture might be a problem. To get the full microporous benefit of the product, the paints or stains should be used on bare wood.

Never work from a new can of paint or stain. Pour sufficient into a paint kettle so that a third of the bristles are covered on the first upright dip. A tip: tap the loaded brush on to the side of the paint kettle, never draw it across the rim as this may cause bubbles to form. Tackle a complete section at a time, be it a panel or strip with a natural joint. The gel-like, non-drip consistency makes the stain easy to apply by brush – no runs, no drips no mess. If part of the door has a metal trim, for example, the surround on an up-and-over garage door, cover the metal with masking tape. The edges of glass in a glazed door can be similarly masked. End grain, edges and joints need special care. If the manufacturer's instructions suggest more than one coat, allow the first to dry thoroughly before rubbing down with fine glass paper. Dust down and, again, wipe off residual dust with a clean cloth dampened with white spirit.

## Treating existing timber

Treatments to existing exterior doors, windows and frames should only be carried out after necessary repairs have been done. Make a careful check of all timber components, especially where two pieces of timber join. A vulnerable part of a window frame, for example, is at the bottom corners where the vertical and horizontal members join to the wooden sill. It is worth a gentle prod with a small metal spike to convince yourself that you don't need to use a DIY wood repair system. Often though, it is only when removing old paint in preparation for redecorating, that this problem is exposed. Pay special attention to the lower joints, not only in window frames, but in doors, door frames, porch timbers, fence posts, wooden gates, greenhouses and conservatories. Unless well protected, all can be subjected to rain-water penetration and eventually wet rot. The cost of professional replacement can be extremely high, so make checks often and, if you do discover a small area that needs attention, attend to it immediately by applying a wood repair system.

If you find a small area of soft wood around a lower joint in a window frame, scrape away only the small area of rot. The soft fibres that are left will be strengthened and reinforced with the special wood-hardener. This is a quick-drying liquid with a resin that binds and hardens the surrounding decayed fibres. The two-part filler is resin-based to provide a very tough surface that can be drilled, screwed, sanded, planed, carved and painted. It bonds and

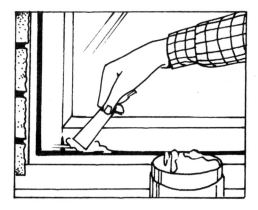

A wood repair system strengthens and reinforces decayed wood. The wood hardener binds and hardens the decayed fibres ready for the tough filler which moves with the wood and doesn't shrink or crack. Wood-preservative tablets are inserted in drilled holes to further protect the wood, which is then ready to be rubbed down and painted.

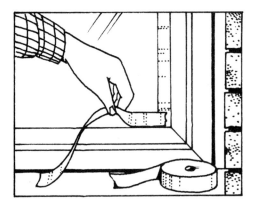

An effective method of getting a perfectly straight line against glass is to use masking tape. Leave a tiny gap so that the paint seals the putty to the glass by about 1/16in (1½mm). Remove the tape before the paint is fully dry.

adheres to the hardener and the surrounding wood but is flexible enough to move with the wood's natural expansion and contraction. Its life is probably longer than the wood itself because it doesn't shrink, crack, split or fall out. As with all timber treatments, be sure that the wood has time to dry out, so that the moisture content is not excessive. An innovative feature of this wood repair system is that further protection is afforded by the insertion of tablets. Wood-preservative tablets are placed into pre-drilled holes around areas where moisture is likely to enter the joinery, for example, at joints, corners and end grain. The drilled holes are then capped with a special wood filler. The tablets are only activated if moisture enters the wood. Then the preservative is released and distributed to the areas most susceptible to rot. The last part of the treatment is the application of two coats of long-life supergloss. The microporous formula of this one-coat paint system resists cracking, peeling and flaking.

Neglected, exposed wood eventually turns grey and the surface loses its texture and lustre, becoming soft and spongy. However, the wood as a whole is still sound, so it is not too late to preserve, stain and protect your fence, shed or cladding, even if it has started to deteriorate. Sufficient preservative chemical must be brushed or sprayed into the wood to prevent fungal or insect attack in that part of the wood which is affected. The more preservative that the wood takes in and the greater the depth of its penetration, the more positive will be its effect. Most preservatives are carried in an organic solvent which enables them to penetrate easily and readily into the timber, providing a high degree of efficiency. They are ideal for DIY application by simple methods like brushing, spraying or dipping. Most preservative compounds are reinforced by the addition of a water repellent which slows down the rate at which wood gets wet. Keeping the wood drier not only helps preserve it but, more importantly, helps control movement thereby reducing irritating nuisances of doors, windows etc. which stick.

## Problem spots

Wherever timber is used externally on a house it is frequently damp, either from the atmosphere or from the ground. Unless it is preserved it will decay. Even supporting timbers covered by cladding, but still subject to moisture-laden air, must be treated with a preservative. Sometimes timbers are unnecessarily subjected to weathering,

An extremely vulnerable area for rain-water penetration into the fabric of a building is any joint between timber and brick. Door frames and window frames need a flexible mastic sealant applied with a cartridge and gun.

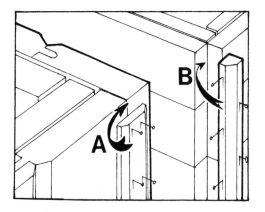

Exterior wooden cladding must be protected by painting or sealing. Joints at external corners on vertical boards as at **A** will have a cover-board to seal — glued and pinned or screwed. Horizontal cladding can meet at a corner as illustrated at **B** and is protected by a tight-fitting batten glued and pinned or screwed.

built in above the window frame and rendered over, improving the elevation too.

There is sometimes an unacceptable risk of timbers decaying due to the nature of design, or standards of workmanship. This is particularly relevant at joints and corners, for example at the corner of a cladded building. Here the method of jointing and the subsequent cover-board are of utmost importance. Rain-water finds the tiniest crack and decay sets in behind the cladding which steadily worsens over one or two winters. The constant banging of a door against a frame weakens and cracks the surrounding mortar joint. Check around all outside door frames for the tiniest crack. A slight discolouring of the timber frame should be enough to spur you into action. Treat the timber with hardening solution and use the best DIY solution to seal the gap. This is a cartridge in a simple gun applicator with an exterior quality mastic sealant. It really is easy

especially when in contact with brickwork. For example, each side of a window frame is fixed to the side bricks of the opening, called the reveals, and needs a mastic sealant to cover and protect the gap between the timber and the brick work. The uppermost edge of a window frame is very vulnerable to weathering but can be protected by a moulded drip. A proprietary metal drip is easily

to master the technique, and worth protecting every door and window frame around your property. It is available in matching colours for every situation.

Other problem spots to keep an eye on are fence posts, garden stakes, seed boxes, window boxes, door thresholds, exposed rafter ends, fascia boards and all timbers in extensions and outbuildings.

## VARNISHING JOINERY

Joinery refers to the skill or craft of a joiner, the person trained and skilled in making finished woodwork. Front doors, windows, porches and conservatories, as well as being functional, can be attractive features enhancing the exteriors of our homes. The tradi-

tional smooth finish to good joinery represents a high degree of craftsmanship. Yacht varnish is ideal for all exterior joinery where a long-lasting high-gloss finish is required to resist the worst extremes of the weather. Never apply varnish when the sun is shining directly on to the joinery. It is also best not to apply it early in the morning or in the later afternoon when dampness in the air could attack it and result in a very dull finish.

Follow the instructions printed on the container of the yacht varnish. Preparation is all important because the smooth finish of good joinery needs to be maintained throughout the protection treatment. A remarkable new resin content helps to prevent cracking, peeling and blistering. It actually flexes with the natural expansion and contraction of wood caused by changes in daily and seasonal temperatures, so it stays strong, sound and high-gloss throughout its extended life.

## DAMP PROBLEMS

Over the years external wall finishes have been subject to designer's whims and to changing ideas of how best to obtain a weathertight construction. All types of wall construction are liable to damp for a number of reasons. Water can creep through the tiniest hairline crack and capillary action will encourage it to seep to an inside surface. If the problem of damp in a wall is not solved it can actually lead to structural deterioration.

Decorations will be spoiled, plaster will lose its adhesion, construction and decorative timber will decay and moulds and rot can develop which can be a health hazard. When wallpaper and interior painted surfaces look and feel damp due to penetration of moisture it is time for immediate action.

Condensation must not be confused with penetrating damp or rising damp, and is dealt with in Chapter 8.

## RISING DAMP

A damp proof course is usually inserted into a house wall about 6in (150mm) above the outside level of the ground. This provides a barrier impervious to moisture, so the cause of a rising damp problem is either the absence or collapse of a damp proof course. The source of the rising damp is the soil or subsoil underneath that wall which as well as a moisture content has decaying plant material, salts, nitrates, chlorides and soil-living animals. Damp rising from the ground and showing on the inside walls of a house is therefore a dilute solution of various materials including nitrates and chlorides. As the damp dries inside a room salts are left behind because they cannot evaporate. These salt deposits on wallpaper and in the plaster surface become the basis for diagnosis of rising damp by a specialist firm.

Salts carried in water from the soil are hygroscopic. This means that they absorb water from the atmosphere and form a solution. The surface of the wall becomes susceptible to the slightest humidity in the atmosphere, so the dampness comes unexpectedly on some days and disappears on others. Another indication of rising damp is a tide mark at a given height above the floor level around the room. An inexpensive DIY damp-meter is available which allows you to monitor the damp conditions around any room.

Efflorescent salts may sometimes appear on walls, but they do not indicate a problem. These salts are always present in building materials and when they are present on the surface of the wall it just indicates that moisture is evaporating from the structure. These are not to be confused with the harmful hygroscopic salts, because they seldom absorb water from the atmosphere. Efflorescence which might have formed on new plaster can be wiped off with a coarse cloth. This is the only treatment that's necessary until the salts cease to appear and the plaster has thoroughly dried out. Never decorate new plaster with paint or paper until it is absolutely dry.

## PENETRATING DAMP

Around the turn of the century an external wall-finish favoured by designers and developers was rendering. A mix of cement, lime and sand was the traditional first coat, followed by a mix of cement, lime shingle or crushed stone and sand. This was thrown on to the wall by hand or with a special trowel. Often this was used externally on solid brick walls as a finish of 'coated' pebble texture.

The skill of the tradesman was obviously very important in the application of both rough cast and pebble dash finishes. Pebble dash was so called because of the use of tiny pebbles or pea shingle (up to ½in (12mm) in diameter) thrown into the top coat of render whilst it was still soft.

Damp problems on the inside walls of an externally rendered surface are due to poor adhesion which causes cracking. The tiniest crack could cause serious problems. Rain-water running down the render will be drawn into the crack by capillary action to saturate the wall behind. In winter ice will form, expand and make the problem worse.

To solve the problem hack off the render that has lost its adhesion right back to where the render is sound. Mix together 1½ parts cement, ½ part lime and 3 parts sand as a finishing coat. Before applying the render, a thin mix of a PVA adhesive should be painted on to the whole of the area to be patched. A little of the PVA in the render mix will help greatly to overcome adhesion problems. Trowel on the mix fairly dry, and obtain a matching finish with either pea shingle or crushed stone. When the area is completely dry, use an exterior sealer before painting to match.

Check at a window opening the thickness of the exterior wall of your house. Solid walls can either be 9in (230mm) or 13½in (350mm) thick. Cavity walls, consisting of two separate 'leaves', with a gap between, are held stable by metal strips known as wall ties. Solid walls are more likely to suffer from ingress of rain-water and penetrating damp than cavity walls. You can also check the construction by looking at the bonding (the way the bricks are laid on the outside of the house). More often you'll see the bricks laid lengthways but if you see a 'header' which is the end of the brick, it usually indicates that the wall is of solid construction. The brick will have been laid end ways on across the wall with an end showing externally and internally. So you can see that if mortar perishes it is very easy for damp to appear inside the house due to capillary action.

Penetrating damp is usually caused by perished or crumbling mortar, in which case it is necessary to rake out the old mortar and repoint. Often you'll find that by raking with an old screwdriver the mortar turns powdery and will crumble. If, on the other hand, a very strong mortar mix was used then cracking will take place and loss of adhesion between the pointing and the building mortar. Rake out to a depth of ¾in (20mm) and square off the recess. If you have a lot to do, a 'plugging' chisel and a club hammer are essential but a bolster chisel and a small club hammer are just as effective. Try not to chip the edges of bricks. Tackle about a square yard (square metre) at a time, brushing out

Form a small pyramid of mortar on the hawk. Practise picking up a 'finger' or slice of mortar on the pointing trowel with a deft upward sweep. Force the mortar into all the vertical joints first.

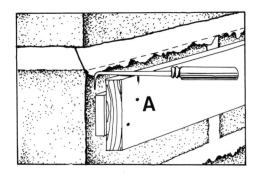

Rake out old and perished mortar from an area of about a square yard (square metre) at a time. Use a plugging chisel and a club hammer to remove the old mortar to a depth of ¾in (20mm) from the vertical joints first, then the horizontal ones. Leave a square clean recess with no damage to brick edges.

After neatening the vertical joints with the trowel, 'strike' or smooth the horizontal ones. The excess mortar hanging at the bottom of the horizontal joints is now made clean and neat by running the 'frenchman' along a batten (**A**) that has two pieces of hardboard nailed to the back. The frenchman is simply made from an old kitchen knife, heated and bent at the tip at right angles. Hold the batten (**A**) with one hand whilst trimming the mortar with the other.

25

all debris and dust from the joints as you go along. Soak the recessed joints and the surrounding brickwork thoroughly before the application of the repointing mortar. You can buy bags of ready-mixed mortar or make your own in the following proportions: 1 part cement, 1 part lime and 6 parts builders' sand. Use the back of a small pointing trowel to pick up a finger of mortar from a small board or hawk. You'll soon get the hang of pushing the mortar firmly into all the upright joints. Hold the board under the work area to catch the excess and falling pieces. Don't bother with striking or shaping the mortar at this stage. Work slowly and carefully to avoid getting the mortar on the face of the bricks. Continue with all the horizontal joints, pressing the mortar deep into the recesses. Allow the mortar to protrude slightly from the face of the brickwork.

Wait for the mortar to firm up before shaping the pointing. Start with the vertical joints holding the trowel at a matching angle. The horizontal joints are shaped in one long continuous movement. If the joint is flush with the bricks, use a small piece of sacking to rub each joint to match. A rubbed or half-round indent joint can be obtained by using a small piece of plastic tube or short length of metal tube. A 'raked' joint shows a

squared off recess, made by running a ½in (12mm) thick lath evenly through the joint and at a consistent depth.

Whatever the area of repointing that you have to tackle, experiment on a small area first. Allied problems of moulds and lichen flourishing in the damp conditions, white crystalline deposits on the surface of the wall, or splashes of plaster or cement should be solved before repointing. Brush off all growth with a stiff bristle brush, then use a fungicidal solution, following the manufacturer's instructions. White deposits or efflorescence are the result of soluble salts in the building materials being drawn to the surface along with the water as the wall dries out. You won't solve this problem by washing the wall because the water and salts will soak back into it. Never decorate over it or damp and salts will be trapped in the wall. When you've repointed and solved the damp problem, the wall will dry out.

Most splashes and blobs of cement or plaster on a wall can be removed with a chisel or a wire brush, provided that the surface is not damaged. Use a proprietary brand of cement remover, following the manufacturer's instructions to remove the residual stains.

## PENETRATING DAMP NEAR WINDOWS AND DOORS

If damp is penetrating around windows and doors, look outside for the cause first. It is very likely that the cement pointing between a wooden frame and brickwork has collapsed because of structural movement. A flexible sealant should be used to seal that joint rather than rigid mortar. Even the

slightest crack will allow ingress of driving rain-water. This will then show as wet patches to the side of the window and especially underneath the window where decorations often suffer.

Persistent dripping from a blocked gutter, a faulty gutter-joint or split rain-water pipe can cause an enormous amount of damage to the structure of the wall and to the internal decorations. Rusting and splitting of an iron rain-water pipe usually happens at the back of the pipe where it can remain undetected for years. Often the back of the pipe is neglected when overhauling or painting.

Constant dousing of the wall with an unusually heavy amount of water can cause mortar to take on the appearance of dough!

In freezing conditions the wet mortar will expand to cause further damage. Check on the outside of the wall for mould forming underneath a suspect gutter and around a cracked downpipe. Inside the house damp patches could appear high up on a bedroom wall or directly behind a cracked pipe. To solve the problem, tackle the cause first. Replace all defective iron rain-water goods (gutters and downpipes) with good-quality plastic ones, and then tackle the pointing. Should damp patches appear in the joint between a ceiling and a wall in an area underneath a parapet wall, the coping

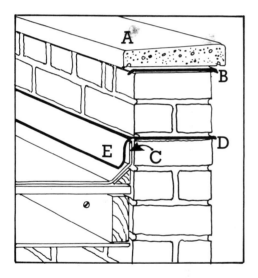

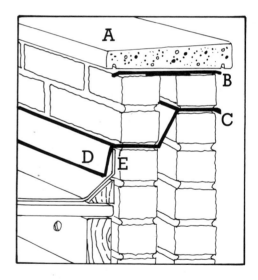

Parapet walls are protected at the top by coping stones (**A**) but are vulnerable because they are exposed on both sides. So it is imperative that adequate protection is provided to prevent rain-water entering the inner walls of the house. Under the coping-stones, ensure that a continuous damp proof course (**B**) is laid. Where a flat roof is built over an extension there must be a 'skirting' or upstand (**C**) of roof covering, covered by a dpc (**D**) in the form of flashing (**E**).

Coping stones (**A**) bedded on to a cavity wall need a piece of slate to bridge the cavity before laying the dpc (**B**). To prevent any rain-water running down inside walls, a continuous dpc is laid at an angle as illustrated (**C**) and flashing (**D**) continues the protection over the upstand or skirting (**E**) of the roof covering.

stones probably either need repointing or rebedding. Coping stones prevent ingress of water to the top of a brick or stone wall, but the coping stones are only as good as the joints between them! If a coping stone has become loose through weathering then it obviously is a danger, as well as being the cause for the dampness. The stones have to be carefully lifted off, the backs cleaned out and the top of the wall prepared for a bed of mortar. You'll probably find a damp proof course of bituminous felt, asphalt or even lead underneath the coping stone. If there is

none, you must first lay one on to a bed of mortar before laying the coping stone on to a further bedding of the same mortar. If a flat roof is fixed to the parapet wall, there must be a flexible damp proof course linking and sealing the roof to the parapet wall. It is usually built into a mortar course about 6in (150mm) above the flat roof and is then dressed over the upstand of skirting formed by the felt on the flat roof lapping up the parapet wall. Check all skirtings and flashings for splits and gaps and treat as described in the section on flat-felt roofs (p.37).

## MAINTAINING BRICK AND STONE WORK

Throughout the history of domestic architecture, it has always been more convenient and economical to use locally produced or manufactured building materials, as bricks, stones, sand and cement are so bulky and weighty.

Bricks were manufactured from locally dug clay, and then fired in the local brick kiln to make them hard-faced and weatherproof. Yet all over the country some bricks suffer, for one reason or another, from flaking or spalling. On one estate in the north of England, every house was seriously affected by this flaking problem. When the surface of bricks shows signs of breaking up, there is always a danger of damp getting through to the inside of the house. The wall facing the prevailing winds and weather is usually the one to suffer damage. On that particular estate the breakdown of the surface of the bricks was on all walls, mainly due to the poor quality of the facing brick.

Often the attractive front elevations of Edwardian houses are decorated with deep

red or ochre bricks. Unfortunately many have a high saturation point to rain-water. If poor quality mortar has been used the problem becomes twofold. At the first sign of frost any moisture which has penetrated the brick surface or the perished mortar surface will freeze. When water freezes it becomes stronger than the building materials surrounding it and it expands. Bricks and mortar have to suffer the consequences! The moral, of course, is continuous vigilance and maintenance, otherwise the processes are repeated until hollows appear in bricks. Spalls then settle into the uneven surface and fungi growth appears.

If a brick in the corner of a building is badly affected and crumbling it needs to be removed completely. Providing you have safe access to the problem area there is a fairly simple DIY method of replacing the brick. A flaking brick on a flat section of wall is just as easy to repair, but in this case it is only necessary to build in half a brick.

You'll need a power drill with hammer

action for both methods. Remember to plug your RCD (Residual Circuit Device) into the socket outlet indoors and then plug in your power tool. With a ⅜in (10mm) masonry bit in the drill, a 2in (50mm) bolster chisel and a 2lb (1 kilo) club hammer you are ready to start the first stage. Make yourself absolutely safe, using safety goggles, a dust mask and gloves.

## FACING BRICKS

Wrap a piece of sticky tape 2in (50mm) from the tip of the drill bit to act as a depth gauge. Drill a series of holes as close together as possible into the mortar surrounding the brick, and into the face of the damaged brick. Using either a cold chisel or a 2in (50mm) bolster chisel and club hammer, remove only the front half of the brick. Use the chisel at an angle to slice at the brick rather than pushing at it. Then there is no risk of it being moved.

The front half must now be replaced with a matching brick cut in half along its length. A DIY powered angle-grinder is the most convenient tool to use. The alternative is to lay the brick on a bed of sand and scribe or incise around the brick by gently tapping with the bolster chisel and hammer. Eventually you'll be able to slice the brick apart. Before cutting with an angle-grinder make sure that the brick is anchored between battens on a piece of board. Push wedges in to

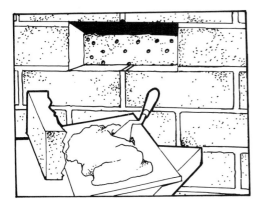

Drill and chop out half the spalled brick and cut a matching brick in half, then spread mortar into the opening. Butter the top of the half-brick and gently ease it into the aperture. Match the pointing either side and brush off excess mortar when almost dry. Apply water repellent when completely dry.

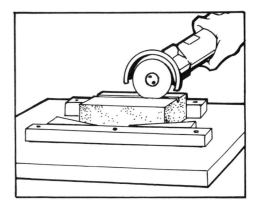

Use safety goggles and gloves. To chop a brick in half, first secure it between battens and two wedges tightly hammered in position. Mark the cut line and use a DIY powered angle-grinder to score along the line to a depth of about ¾in (20mm). A few taps with a bolster will successfully split the brick.

hold it fast. Cut along the half-way line, using two or three fairly quick strokes. Turn it over and repeat the process. The chisel and hammer will now split it in two.

Hold it in place to check for fit. You'll need ½in (12mm) of mortar around and behind the half-brick. Dampen the opening and the surrounding brick edges. Mix the mortar dry in these proportions: 6 parts washed sand, 1 part cement, 1 part lime. Add water, continue to mix until a uniform colour is obtained and a small piece retains its shape when squeezed in the hand. Trowel it into the opening, butter the top of the half-brick and gently ease it into place. Fill up the gaps and point up the mortar joint to match the existing pointing.

## CORNER BRICKS

It is quite safe to remove a corner brick by drilling into the mortar. Drill only to a depth of 4in (100mm). (Wrap a piece of tape around the masonry bit to use as a depth gauge.) Drill the holes close together so that the minimum of heavy hammering with the bolster chisel is needed to loosen the brick.

Having cleaned out the corner opening and chopped away all traces of old mortar, dampen all faces and spread mortar on the sides and bottom of the opening. Butter a brick on the top and slide it into position, lining it up properly. Match the pointing and, when dry, paint a colourless water repellent over the whole wall.

When loose the brick should slide out quite easily. By gently chiselling the residue of mortar, clean up the hole. Allow as little debris as possible to fall into the cavity.

At this stage if you can't get a matching brick there is a simple DIY solution for a replacement – simply clean up and show the other side of the brick that you have removed. The flaking part will be hidden and protected from further damage by being turned around and sealed.

Dampen the replacement area. Mix 4 parts building sand to 1 part cement, then add water which has been mixed with a plasticizer. (The label of the plasticizer will carry full instructions.) Bed the brick on to the same thickness of mortar as the surrounding pointed joints. Before inserting the brick, trowel mortar on to the side bricks and on to the top of the replacement brick, gently ease it into position and line it up. You'll find that the mortar strap joint (the new mortar joint linking to the firm pointing either side) will be fairly easy to match by tilting the trowel to the same angle and gently drawing it along the mortar course. Any mortar on the surrounding brickwork can be brushed off with a soft handbrush.

A wall that has a flaking brick or stone is a neglected wall. Check all the pointing on that section of the wall too, because the slightest crack can allow water penetration. (*See* pp.24–6.)

Having replaced and repaired bricks and mortar, you'll undoubtedly be pleased with the attractive result. To further protect that elevation, apply a DIY Brick and Stone Sealer by brush or spray. This colourless liquid, absorbed by bricks and mortar, does not change the colour but adds years of protection to the wall.

## STONE

Stone withstands the ravages of time and weather. Natural stone, hewn into blocks for building, has an attractive texture, is durable and is aesthetically pleasing. Most stone used in domestic buildings has been quarried locally. Stones used in buildings are mostly of a regular form and semi-dressed, which means the surface is roughly cut or chiselled. Fully-dressed stone has flat even faces so that tight joints can be made and the elevation face dressed flat.

Some building stones, including limestones and sandstones, can be seriously affected by weathering. Spalling can take place quite seriously on a wall subjected to driving westerly winds and rain. It is pos-

sible to carry out the same form of repair as for a spalling brick. After the front half of a spalling stone has been removed to help overcome the problem of adhesion of the new front-half facing stone, use a PVA solution all over the recess and on the back of the half-replacement stone. The solution should be 50% PVA adhesive and 50% water. Never use rain-water, pond-water or sea-water for mixing any building materials. These could have an acid, nitrate or chloride content which could adversely affect the constituents of the mix. Press the facing stone into a bed of mortar and point up to match the surrounding area.

## REPAIRING AND MAINTAINING PATHS AND DRIVES

Well-designed paths and drives should provide attractive means of access to your house. The original construction work and materials should provide a firm, flat surface which allows rain-water to drain off easily. It should be easy to keep clean and treated with a fungicide to keep it free of moss and algae. Often the soft landscaping of lawns, plants and shrubs is given priority over the maintenance of the hard landscaping, namely patios, walls, paths and drives.

Laying paths and drives is probably the most costly outlay in the area surrounding your house. There are three reasons why you should aim for as high a standard of maintenance as possible – safety, aesthetics and economics. There are simple but effective methods of solving the problems of crumbling edges, cracks and pot-holes in paths and drives.

A drive or path should not just be a means of reaching the house or crossing the garden, it should also provide an attractive feature surrounded by soft landscaping. For these reasons different materials are used for paths and drives. Over the years concrete has been a popular choice because of its versatility. For drives it can be laid in panels of different sizes and patterns separated by expansion joints of another material. Aggregates or chippings sprinkled into the almost dry surface will provide a non-slip finish. Another method of providing a non-slip surface is to brush it as it dries. But concrete can and will deteriorate if it is not laid to conform to good building principles. Poorly prepared paths and drives of concrete can pose problems ranging from cracking to subsidence. A minor problem caused by excessive use of a steel float or trowel when the concrete is laid is a constantly dusty surface. If this is allowed to persist the surface layer will show signs of cracking and possibly crumbling. Rain-water will penetrate or lay in puddles on the surface and freeze in icy conditions. The result is further breaking up of the surface compounded by constant usage. If a path or drive is at that stage, read the repair section! It is simple, though, to prevent a dusty surface from deteriorating any further, by using a proprietary brand of concrete sealer, available in most DIY super-centres. Apply only after brushing away all dust and treating all moss and algae.

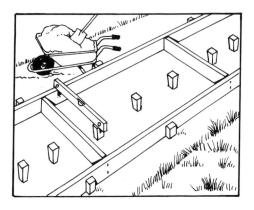

Drives and paths need proper planning, with form-work laid level with pegs to maintain a good level surface. Check each peg with a spirit level. Compacted soil or, better still, 4in (100mm) hardcore compacted with a plate vibrator, supports the concrete. Working in bays makes the job easier to handle and expansion joints are formed in the process. Make a slight fall so that rain-water runs away.

All paths and drives should have their edges protected by bricks set in concrete or by edging stones. Without this protection, edges break up, especially in winter when water penetrates and ice forms. If cracks appear at the edge of a concrete drive, chop back to form a hard edge. Lay a board upright supported by pegs. Dig out as far as the hardcore and use a PVA mix before filling and levelling with concrete.

## EDGES

A drive or path laid with concrete should be constructed in sections with contraction joints between. A long concrete path should have joints at 6 to 10ft (1.5 to 3m) intervals depending on the subsoil. Ideally, all paths and drives should have protection at their edges. 2ft (½m) lengths of nosed concrete edging strips can be used on a long straight run, but bricks are more attractive. Edging supports must be laid in a good bed of concrete to firmly hold against heavy traffic. Proprietary strips of galvanized metal can also be used.

If the edge of a path has no protection and has begun to crumble, use a bolster chisel and club hammer to cut away the edges of the crack. If there is no hard core supporting the concrete, undercut around the area for a couple of inches, so that the repair concrete will support the cut edges. The new concrete will bond to the old more readily and permanently if a PVA adhesive is brushed on to the repair. Mix the PVA admixture to the concrete mix as well, to make it less susceptible to frost damage. The manufacturer's instructions will cover both these applications. Use a length of timber to extend past the patch repair held firmly to the edge of the path supported with pegs driven into the ground.

Mix together, dry first, 1 part cement, 3 parts sharp sand and 2 parts coarse aggregate. If the surface texture of the existing path shows little or no signs of aggregate or pebbles, you can change the mixture to 1 part cement, 4 parts sharp sand and 1 part aggregate. A clean ice-cream tub is ideal for measuring out the quantities when only small amounts are required. Form a depression in the dry mix and pour in some water, to which has been added the PVA admixture. Mix together with a shovel until you get an even colour. Add very little water at a time to keep the mix firm, not sloppy. Shovel the mix into the repair area and force it under the chopped edges with a piece of timber. Continue to fill, prodding into it well to eliminate air bubbles. Level it to the existing surface and try to match the texture.

After laying, concrete has no holding strength for about five days. It is a mistaken belief that concrete actually dries out and that the quicker it dries the quicker it hardens. Paradoxically, moisture is essential to the curing process which can take up to a month. That is why you'll see a tradesman dampening down concrete with a watering can and covering it with a plastic sheet to help retain its moisture.

## REPAIRING CRACKS

A fairly straight crack across a path or drive is usually caused by movement or subsidence in the ground. If there is no crumbling either side of the crack, use an exterior quality mastic filler to prevent water ingress. Cracks of this nature should be left for at least a year so the possible worsening can be monitored.

Cracks with a crazy-paving look need immediate attention. Grass and weeds thrive in conditions where a supply of moisture is always present. Chip away at the crack with a bolster chisel until you get a hard edge. After undercutting the cracked area, treat with a weed killer following the manufacturer's instructions. Then fill, in the same way as for crumbling edges. Small repairs can be carried out simply with a bag of readi-mix and a cement colourizer (if needed).

## REPAIRING DEPRESSIONS

All paths and drives should be laid with a very slight slope or fall away from a building. This prevents water collecting and minimizes the risk of accidents due to ice. Depressions can form, however, by subsidence, or even poor workmanship at the levelling stage! All depressions must be hacked out to allow a minimum of 1in (25mm) of new concrete to be laid. If the depression is deep and the thickness of concrete too little to allow use of chisel and club hammer, then break up the depression completely. Excavate as for crumbling edges and fill in the same way.

## PRE-CAST CONCRETE PAVING SLABS

Pre-cast concrete paving slabs are being made by manufacturers as the the demand grows. A standard range of shapes and sizes is available cast in moulds to produce varying surface finishes. Many finishes resemble natural stone and are available in subtle blends of colours, so it shouldn't be difficult to walk into your DIY Garden Centre to obtain a matching slab if you need to replace a broken one. Cast concrete paving slabs can make visually appealing and attractive paths. However, two factors can contribute to slabs breaking. One is the nature and thinness of the material and the other is poor preparation and laying. Weak points in a path always show up in an area where there is a lot of foot traffic. Between the front door and the garden gate the most common repair is likely to be the removal and re-laying of a rocking slab or one that has dipped through subsidence. The base for a slabbed path can be as little as 2in (50mm) of sharp sand laid on compacted soil. A far better finish is possible by laying a sub-base of compacted hard core to a depth of 4in (100mm). A plate vibrator ensures that the hard core is firm, flat and very compacted.

The slabs are laid on the compacted sand one at a time, on a bed of mortar mixed 1 part cement to 4 parts sand. The mortar can either be laid on in five blobs or a continuous layer. Broken slabs must be replaced and re-laid on the same base of mortar. An undamaged slab that is rocking can be lifted very simply by levering it with a spade. Take care not to let it fall back on itself because it will shatter. A cracked slab can be broken up into smaller pieces with a bolster chisel and club hammer making them easier to lever out without disturbing the surrounding slabs. To re-lay a slab, add more sand at compacted level with the existing. Mix a small amount of mortar 1 part cement to 5 parts sand but keep it fairly dry. A thin mix of mortar will not support the slab. Gauge sufficient mortar so that the slab will rest about ½in (12mm) above the existing path. With a batten of wood laid across the slab tap the batten to level it. After four days a dry mix of sand and cement can be used to fill in the joints.

## TARMAC PATHS AND DRIVES

If a tarmac drive or path crumbles at the edges and does not have edging strips it could be a very costly business to replace the path or drive when water has undermined the whole area. Bricks or pre-cast concrete edging strips set into concrete create an attractive edge but more importantly retain the edges, preventing the tarmac crumbling. Ideally, tarmac should be laid on a concrete base. All tarmac surfacings should have retaining edging bricks or blocks. It is worth

excavating a channel in which a bed of concrete can then be laid to support the edging pieces. Extra concrete can provide a buttress at the back of the edging strip to prevent outward thrust.

Fortunately, there is a very simple DIY method of solving the problem of crumbling

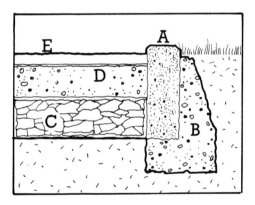

Drive surfaced with tarmac. Sectional illustration shows how an edging stone (**A**) is set in concrete (**B**), forming a buttress to protect a drive. The hardcore (**C**) is laid to a thickness of 4in (100mm), well compacted before sand or old plaster is used to blind it so that the 3in (75mm) of concrete (**D**) is supported. The tarmac (**E**) is laid and rolled to give a long-lasting and durable surface.

Should a tarmac path or drive show signs of wear and develop pot-holes it is an easy job to resurface or fill holes with a proprietary brand of cold cure tarmac sold in bags. (To resurface a tarmac drive use fresh bitumen emulsion in which is embedded stone chippings). For filling a pot-hole, cut out to expose the hardcore, paint with the bitumen emulsion supplied, fill with the 'warmed' tarmac and roll, using a watering can to keep the roller wet.

tarmac. Bags of red or black tarmac are available from your DIY Supercentre. A 55lb (25 kilo) bag of cold cure tarmac should cover 6 square feet (½ square metre) laid 1in (25mm) thick. If your drive has stone chippings embedded in the tarmac, use the separate bag of chippings included in the main sack. Keep the tarmac warm overnight and it will be ready for use in the morning.

Remove all loose and crumbling tarmac and loose hard core. Compact the subsoil and re-lay the hard core adding sufficient to bring it up to the correct height. Firmly compact it with a club hammer. Pour in sufficient of the tarmac to bring it level with the drive. For large areas, a garden roller kept wet will compact the tarmac by rolling in all directions. For small areas of about a square foot (300mm × 300mm) tamp with a wet 4inch × 2inch (100mm × 50mm) piece of timber, about 2ft (½m) long. Fresh tarmac should be left for a couple of days before walking or driving on it.

Pot-holes in tarmac must be cut out completely. Cut the sides vertically and hack out all loose tarmac and hard core. Well-compacted hard core can be left and added to. Hammer the top surface of the hard core to break it up into smaller pieces which makes a firmer bed for the tarmac. Paint the whole of the repair with the bitumen emulsion manufactured for this purpose. Within a short while it turns black and only then should you fill the hole with a minimum of 1in (25mm) tarmac. Roll it or tamp it level using a watering can to dampen the surface.

Small pieces and splashes of tarmac can cling to clothing and to the soles of boots. Dust will then cling to the particle of tarmac. If clothes are not checked and working boots not cleaned with a solvent, carpets and floor-coverings can be stained. Take great care that tools and protective clothing are cleaned with the manufacturer's recommended solvent. Gloves should be worn whilst working with this material.

If a vehicle has to be left standing on a tarmac drive, make use of a spillage tray whenever possible. Petrol and oil spilled on the surface of a tarmac drive or path will soften it, causing problems. Depressions will occur, turning puddles to skid pads in winter, and the ice will expand inside the surface of the tarmac and break it up.

## CRAZY PAVING

A path made of crazy paving is the easiest to repair. An area of stones is laid in a random pattern so a broken stone is easily lifted, cleaned up and re-laid. Crazy paving can be laid in two ways either on a bed of mortar on the sand base or straight on to the sand with the joints pointed up with mortar.

Use a cold chisel and club hammer to break up the pointing all around the broken stone. Take care as you lift out the broken stone that it does not laminate, or split into thin layers. If the stones are not natural then this will not present a problem. Clean up the whole of the repair area and check that the pieces will fit back allowing the broken pieces to have joints between them. Match the base with sand and re-lay the stones, on mortar if necessary. Tap them level and repoint to match the surrounding area.

Paths with quite distinctive patterns can be laid using bricks in different bonds. The traditional herring-bone pattern is attractive but may give problems at the edge of the path because small triangular pieces have to be cut as infill as the bricks are laid diagonally. If they are not firmly bedded and have no protection at the edges then problems will arise. Rocking or broken bricks in any pattern can be replaced very easily because they are not usually bedded in mortar. Try to obtain matching bricks as replacements and if only a few have to be cut, use an angle-grinder. Wear goggles and gloves to cut bricks which should be either secured in a bed of sand or wedged between timbers. An electric angle-grinder must be protected with an RCD at the plug end of the cable in the house.

## FLAT-FELT ROOF PROBLEMS

One of the most common problems in our homes in the past has been leaking flat-felt roofs. At the first sign of a ceiling stain and drips of rain-water we rush for a bowl to catch the drips. Then, when the storm is over, out comes the proverbial tin of 'black-stuff' and the trowel with a build-up of mastic, usually wrapped in newspaper, and a quick but temporary repair is effected. Unfortunately, this type of repair will never last: proper preparation has been neglected and the mastic will lose its adhesion. So, out comes the 'black-stuff' again! Meanwhile the roof is deteriorating further and inevitably a full roof-repair job is looming.

Statutory regulations cover the construction of flat-felt roofs. These are designed to ensure that the building is safe and weatherproof. Achieving this, of course, depends on two factors, as the job is only as good as, firstly, the builder's knowledge and expertise and, secondly, the materials used.

Heavy joists support the flat timber covering. The ceiling boards are nailed to the underside of the joists. Between the two boards there should be thermal and damp barriers; it is also very important that each space is ventilated to prevent condensation. On top of the roof boards is fixed the weatherproofing material, which more often than not is layers of felt. The regulations call for three layers, the top of which is a coded mineral felt. Good building practice is, however, the all-important factor in this construction! This type of building work – which is difficult to survey or investigate – can be prone to shoddy workmanship and unprofessional building practices, which in turn results in degeneration through poor design and skimped work and materials.

In this climate of ours in the UK we experience extremes of temperature and humidity. The frequent changes of heating and cooling, even over short periods, is one cause of the breakdown of roofing materials. All materials come under stress during this cycle of movement. Moisture, even that carried in the air, can cause twisting and warping of timber, as well as cracking, which occurs with drying out and shrinkage. The constant heat of the sun on a felt roof can cause the bitumen to slip and creep but, more importantly ultraviolet rays degrade bitumen and mastic coverings. Felts become brittle,

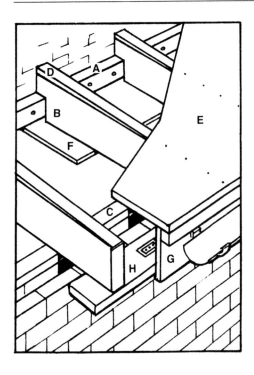

cracks appear, blisters swell up and split. All contribute to our leaking roof problems.

Statutory regulations cover the principles of construction of flat roofs to ensure that the building is safe and weatherproof. A typical construction is shown. A heavy timber ledger is bolted to the house wall. Joists are notched and fixed to the ledger and to a timber 'wall-plate' resting on the cavity wall supporting the roof. Wedge-shaped 'furring' pieces on the top of the joists give the 'fall' or slope. Timber 'decking' is fixed above the joists and plasterboard ceiling below. A vertical fascia board supports the gutter and with the horizontal soffit board encloses the structure. Small vents in the soffit provide roof ventilation.

## WATERPROOFING SYSTEMS

The advantages of a flat-felt roof are the low cost, the speed and ease of installation and the water-repellent characteristics of felt. However, neglect over a period of time can mean the total replacement of all the roofing components. Calling in a roofing contractor can involve resurfacing with hot applied bitumens and tars which can prove very costly. Of course, these processes do call for professional skills and specialist equipment.

The life span of traditionally used bituminous and rubber-based products for domestic flat roofs has always been limited and manufacturers of DIY products have long been aware of this. Industrial and commercial buildings have been better served;

for years the building industry has had the advantage of a specially formulated liquid which, when applied to roofs, cures and forms a continuous weatherproof membrane. Researchers and chemists have now found a roofing compound for the DIY trade, which is easy to apply, long lasting and economical. One manufacturer has produced a liquid rubber waterproofing system which can be used on balconies, boat decks, sheds and felt roofs. The instructional leaflet carries an introduction which claims the product has 'high tensile strength; durability and storage life stability; the selection of the highest grade raw materials provide the quality so essential for consistently good on-site performance; offers unrivalled reliability.'

Well, there *are* rivals and one is a liquid flexible reinforced plastic about which the manufacturer makes similar claims!

### Rubber waterproofing system

This is designed to enable the membrane to adhere to practically any type of roofing material provided that it is correctly prepared. It can be applied to cover a complete roof or as a patch repair. Before starting, clean surrounding surfaces. Remove all loose chippings and dust. Use a fungicidal liquid to rid surfaces of algae or growth, then wash down thoroughly and allow to dry. Liquid rubber systems cannot be used on damp surfaces. Preparation also includes ensuring that the felt is properly fixed to the roofing timber and that no silicone repellants are present. Fill cracks with the mastic filler. Cut a star shape in blisters, fill with

mastic and flatten with felt tacks. Deep depressions must also be filled, where puddles of water are likely to form and freeze.

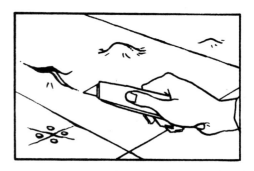

Check carefully for blisters and 'lifting'. Use a trimming knife to open the blisters with star cuts. Tap the felt flat and use large-headed galvanized clout nails to hold the felt down in preparation for the first application of the mixture of plastic and hardener. Treat any loose and lifting areas in the same manner.

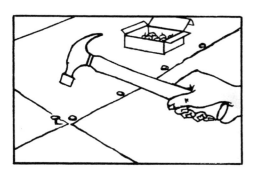

After preparing the roof surface with fungicidal solution and detergent, wash down thoroughly. Check now for open seams and splits caused by the action of the sun or movement in the structure. Nail down all openings but use only galvanized clout nails.

The membrane is extremely pliable and can be used very successfully to repair and protect upstands. Once in place and given a second application of the liquid coating, it will withstand all weathering and the shedding of rain-water down the wall.

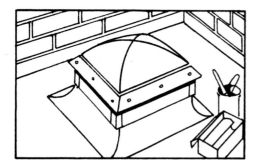

For repairs to internal or external corners, valley-gutters, joints to chimney-stacks or to free-standing protuberances like vents, a liquid water-proofing repair kit is the ideal problem solver.

Cracks and joints that are liable to movement need careful attention. Pour the liquid rubber into the crack or joint until flush with the surface. Use the primer, let it dry, then apply more liquid rubber. Use wide strips of reinforcing woven-fabric scrim material and lay it into the liquid rubber. Immediately apply a further coat. Upstands, flashings and valleys can be made stronger by the same method.

Treat all splits, cracks, blisters and faults as described above. Use only galvanized tacks to hold down difficult areas. Paint on the special primer to cover the area completely and obtain a uniform coating. Wait for 48 hours then apply the liquid rubber again in exactly the same way. Two top coats are recommended to minimize the risk of missed areas, pin holes or spreading the first coat too thinly. The second top coat should be applied within 24 hours of the first one being dry enough to walk on. Never try to dilute the liquid rubber. Measure the areas to be treated; the instruction leaflet will tell you exactly how much to buy to cover that particular area. If you finish only part of the job in one day there is no problem restarting next morning, as long as you keep the untreated part dry and, when restarting, overlap the already treated part by at least 6in (150mm). Although this liquid rubber system does not degrade with ultraviolet light, long bursts of heat from the sun can affect any bituminous coatings which may have been applied beneath the top coat of felt.

Chippings are not strictly necessary on this type of roof finish but they can be applied if the surface is not subject to foot traffic, and this will minimize any adverse affects by solar heat. There are paints with solar reflective finishes on the market, which also can be applied to this liquid rubber roof finish.

Because the liquid rubber and special primer cure by reaction with moisture in the air, an opened tin is liable to skin formation on the top of the liquid, so try to buy only enough for the job in hand. The obvious rules apply as to health and safety: wear suitable clothing and, especially, protective gloves, keep the products out of reach of children and don't empty them into the kitchen sink! A cautionary word to finish; the special primer and the clean up fluid are flammable liquids, although the liquid rubber is not.

### Plastic waterproofing system

An alternative to the liquid rubber is to use another roofing system that the manufacturer claims is totally different to anything else on the market. The product is presented as a distress purchase for the DIYer who must repair his leaking roof as quickly as possible with a minimum of fuss. Everything that you need is in the kit except the

To ensure complete success using the repair kit, prepare a clean, dry surface. Treat for fungal growth and moss, wash down and dry thoroughly. Follow the instructions on the packet and the roof surface will be hard but flexible within 3 to 4 hours. Work in small areas only but overlap the membrane if you have to continue next day.

paintbrush, and scissors for cutting the membrane. It's clean and simple to use and is formulated especially for the enthusiastic DIYer (although the skill factor in application is minimal), so if you own a ladder, you can fix your roof. This roofing system is formulated to be permanent once applied and is unaffected by ageing, the action of the sun, or freezing and thawing cycles. It remains flexible and has the ability to absorb thermal and moisture movement even, it is claimed, at sub-zero temperatures. A single-coat application is sufficient and the marvellous thing is that it hardens in two to three hours depending upon the ambient temperature. There is no need for any fillers but bumps and blisters should be cut and nailed flat. As before, sweep everything off the roof and make sure it's dry and free from any oil, grease or silicone. As long as there is not going to be rain for three hours, you can finish the job!

Mix the liquid plastic with the hardener and liberally brush on to the required area. Place the membrane on to the wet resin and position correctly. Using the same solution, paint over the membrane until it's completely saturated. Any storms after three hours and no drips or leaks will be found inside your house! With this product it will take you only hours rather than days to overcome all the problems associated with leaking flat-felt roofs.

# CHAPTER THREE

# DECORATING

## PAINTING

Mastering the technique of using a brush or roller comes with practice. Paint must be transferred from a tin on to a wall or a wooden surface and spread evenly with a brush or roller leaving no apparent joins.

## PAINTING TECHNIQUES

### Brushes

Dip the brush into the paint to cover a third of the bristles and tap it on the side of the paint kettle. Apply the paint to wood in the direction of the grain. Lightly cross the paint at right angles and finish by stroking back from the unpainted area into the painted area very lightly. This is called laying off. Never draw the brush along from wet paint to where fresh paint is to be applied. If the brush is overloaded or the paint spread too thinly, brush marks will certainly show.

### Rollers

Even when painting with a roller, you first need to paint the edges, such as the joins between walls and ceilings, with a brush. Then pour the paint into a tray without overloading it and dip the roller into the well of the tray, rolling backwards to the top of the tray. Lift the roller, take it half-way down the tray and roll backwards again to even out the paint on the roller. Apply sparingly to surface, using a criss-cross motion to obtain an even spread.

## PAINTING PROBLEMS

Even though painting and decorating techniques are not difficult to master, lack of preparation can lead to disappointing results. There are basic principles which just cannot be avoided. A good professional finish depends upon adequate preparation, which is 50 per cent of the time spent on the total job.

### Dimpled paint

To avoid the problem of dimpled paint, a room has to be well ventilated while you are painting, with no dampness in the air. If condensation forms as the paint dries, which is a fault common to oil-based paints, it may be that warm, moist air has come into contact with the surface that you're painting which might be very cold. Another reason for dimpled paint may be that the surface being painted has not been properly prepared. All surfaces must be firm, with no loose paint or powdery plaster, degreased, absolutely clean and keyed to receive the paint.

## Grey streaks

Baffling grey streaks appearing mysteriously on your freshly painted surface are caused by dust. Unless you've been absolutely scrupulous in the cleaning preparation, dust will be picked up on the brush from the tops of doors, key holes, the corners of window frames, latch-keepers and ledges. Reddish-brown streaks appearing in paint are usually the result of rust from the inside of an old half-used tin of paint.

## Runs and rivers

It is not always easy to see runs and rivers forming on a vertical surface when painting in the wrong light. When dry, runs show up very badly especially in a side light. These occur if the brush is overloaded or if not enough time is taken to 'lay off' the paint. (*See* painting techniques, p.42) Runs and rivers have to be removed either with a jelly paint stripper or by muscle power with a medium to fine glass paper.

## Blisters

Blisters appearing on a painted wall can be the result of painting on to a damp surface or of using emulsion paint on a wall previously painted with a gloss paint, which has not been properly prepared. To avoid this problem, a wall has to be thoroughly dry, flat, firm and degreased. A stabilizing primer should be used to fix or bind powdery or flaking plaster wall surfaces.

## Slow drying paint

Paint that is still wet long past its recommended drying time has probably been applied in cold weather. It can also be the result of painting over wax crayon marks, splashed candle grease or a greasy surface, for example around a cooker, that has not been properly prepared. The answer is to strip off the paint, clean it back to a firm base and use a solvent to degrease the area.

## Rough paint surface

Finished paintwork should look fresh and be satin smooth to the touch. Small pimples or bittiness on the surface of new paintwork show up when dust is trapped beneath the paint film. The remedy is to rub down the surface to an extra smooth finish using a 'wet and dry' treatment (silicone-carbide paper, wetted). Use the finest grade of 'wet and dry' to gently abrade the surface, and always feather the edges so that a ridge is not left around the rubbed down area and it is left absolutely smooth to the touch. Finally clean off with a rag dampened with white spirit before repainting. After having rubbed down any surface in preparation for painting, especially if you have used glass paper, never just finish off with a dusting brush – always wipe the surface with a clean cloth moistened with white spirit.

## Crazing

There are a number of reasons why crazing appears on a painted surface. It can result simply from applying one type of paint over another which is not compatible. If two different types of paint have been used together the first coat will expand and contract at a different rate to the top coat, causing it to crack. If a top coat of an oil-based paint has been applied to an undercoat that is not completely dry and hard, then crazing can also occur. You'll also see it on surfaces that have not been properly rinsed of the cleaning material used in the preparation. If the crazing is extensive then the entire surface must be stripped down and repainted. In small areas simply rub down with 'wet

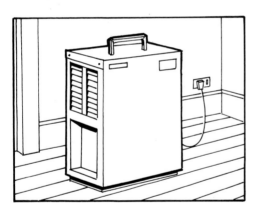

A dehumidifier will not only rid the building materials of all excess moisture but will extract moisture from furnishings too. It combats condensation by drawing the moisture laden air into the specially built unit which condenses the water vapour and fills the container with water to be emptied. The dry air is then heated and convected back to the room.

and dry' paper in preparation for a new top coat.

## Efflorescence

Efflorescence is a white deposit of salts found on the surface of plaster, concrete, brick or stone and caused by alkaline salts being brought to the surface in the drying out process. It is mostly found in new houses and should be removed by rubbing with rough sacking. Hire a dehumidifier to help the drying process, which will speed up the 'bringing-to-the-surface' of the salts. Once the wall has dried out, clean off, rub down and apply an alkali-resistant primer before decorating. Follow the manufacturer's instructions exactly.

## Flaking

Flaking can occur if efflorescence (*see above*) has been allowed to continue its migration to the wall surface after paint has been applied. Painting on a damp or contaminated surface, applying emulsion over gloss paint or painting on a powdery surface can also result in flaking. To remedy, strip off all loose and flaking paint and thoroughly sand the whole of the wall. Clean off, allow the wall to dry and then apply a coat of primer sealer.

Blisters and flaking on exterior painted timber are unsightly and the direct result of poor preparation. If timber has not been allowed to dry out before paint is applied the moisture will try to escape when the summer sun warms up the wood. Moisture will cause lack of adhesion, resulting in the paint lifting off and flaking. Sometimes shoddily prepared timber has been given a coat of emulsion before a top coat of gloss. This, of course, will not last any time and flaking will occur. Blisters can also be caused by moisture being trapped between the wood and the paint surface. More often than not, though, blisters will be found over a knot in the wood. It is essential to use shellac knotting on all knots and resinous areas to prevent resin escaping and bleeding through the paintwork. To overcome the problem, prepare as for new wood by removing the paint, rubbing down and allowing the surface to dry thoroughly.

Before repainting a door or a window frame, it might not be necessary to strip all the paint from the door or frame. The rule is that any surface to be repainted has to be properly prepared, but if paint is absolutely sound and hard, with no cracks, gaps, flaking or pitting, then all you need to do is to use sandpaper to provide a 'key', so that the paint will hold.

Always use a paint kettle and not the paint tin.

Never use a screwdriver to open a tin of paint or the lid will become distorted and will not protect the paint from drying out. Hooked paint tin openers are available from DIY stores, but a hook-end bottle opener is just as effective!

Never store a half-empty tin of paint upside down – the skin formed will cause problems later on. When the paint is stirred the skin will break and lumps form in the paint.

To prevent a skin forming on paint, cut a piece of thin polythene to drop onto its surface.

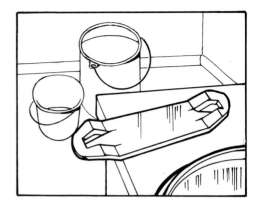

To open a tin of paint, use a can opener upside down with the point upwards. Place it on the edge of the tin and gently lever. Never use paint straight from the tin. Avoid problems by pouring 2–3in (50–75mm) into a plastic kettle – easy to clean afterwards because even hard paint cracks and falls off by flexing the plastic!

The brush wrap shown preserves the action part of the brush so that it can be used straight from the wrap. The Brush Clean uses the solvent in the paint itself to clean the paint from the brush, which is then washed out under the tap. Both are non-toxic, odourless and nonflammable.

## PATCH PLASTERING AND REPAIRING PLASTERWORK

No amount of paint or wallpaper can cover bad patch plastering! Some wall areas suffer badly, especially in older houses. Constantly banging a front door will eventually dislodge plaster that has lost its adhesion. Damp patches under windows result in blown plaster. Chiselling out channels for electrical cables leaves an unsightly ridge if the repair is carelessly done. Repairing holes and channels, whether purposely made or the result of neglect, is now much easier. The new one-coat DIY plasters on the market make it simple to repair small holes and cracks in a plaster wall in preparation for painting or wallpapering. With a tub of ready-mixed one-coat plaster, it is just as easy to fill and level a 3in wide × 1in deep (75mm × 25mm) floor to ceiling channel, as an area of blown plaster measuring a foot across!

## PREPARATION

First of all, hack away all loose plaster to give a firm edge around the whole area. Brush away dust and debris and then dampen the area, including the undercut edges. If you are working in a room where there is a carpet be certain to cover the whole of the adjacent area (and that between the work area and the door) with a floor covering. The smallest piece of plaster dropped on to the floor and carried by a shoe can make stain marks elsewhere. Have a bucket of clean water and a clean, soft 4in (100mm) brush close by, as well as a large steel filler-knife (ideal for applying the plaster) and a straight edge of smooth prepared timber, slightly longer than the longest measurement of the repair. A piece of hardboard or plastic sheeting pulled tight to the skirting board underneath the repair will catch any dropped plaster and keep it clean for re-use (if retrieved immediately).

## APPLYING THE PLASTER

With some plaster on the centre of the hawk, and the hawk immediately under the work area, apply small amounts of plaster to one edge, pressing firmly to form a key. Continue to fill until the whole area is covered and slightly proud of the surrounding plaster. Starting at the bottom of the patch, use the straight edge in small scissor movements to straighten the patch and level it with the wall surface. If there are hollows, now is the time to fill them. Continue to fill hollows and lift off excess plaster until you are satisfied that the patch is true and level with all the edges. Leave it to stiffen for the recommended time indicated on the tub. When your finger leaves no impression, it is time to dampen the surface with a special close-textured sponge, as supplied in the kit. Now use the plastic spreader from the kit or a steel float (trowel), held at an angle close to the wall, to polish the dampened plaster. Use a fairly strong action, vertically and horizontally, but do keep the work and the float wet all the time. This action is most

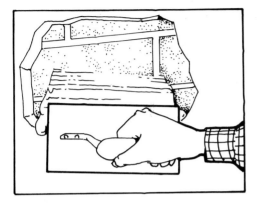

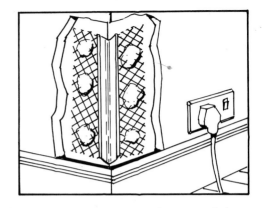

Chisel away the patch of blown plaster to a hard edge. Apply the plaster to the lower edge firmly, keying it into the undercut edge which has been dampened. Build up the whole area, slightly proud of the wall surface. Use a straight edge in a scissors movement to flatten the patch. Leave to stiffen. Use a damp sponge over the almost dry plaster then with firm strokes polish the surface with the steel float (trowel).

A corner that is damaged is easily repaired by using a plasterer's metal corner beading set in position with blobs of plaster and plastered over using a one-coat plaster. Hold a batten against the corner, vertically so that one side can be plastered up the batten which coincides exactly with the corner of the wall. Remove the batten and do the same to the other side.

satisfying: you'll actually see the polished surface drying out as you work firmly on the plaster. Stand back to admire your work, but you won't be able to admire the final decorative finish until the plaster has dried completely.

Where an external corner of a plaster wall has been chipped, it is just as easy to repair. If a long piece of the corner has been knocked off or broken away, chip back the plaster leaving an area to be covered about 3in (75mm) each side of the corner. Buy a length of plasterer's metal corner beading; cut it to length and set it into the corner with blobs of one-coat plaster. Hold a straight edge against the top and bottom of the corner and work the bead parallel to the straight edge and aligned with the original plaster surfaces either side of it. Use masonry nails to hold a piece of timber as a guide against one face so that you can apply the one-coat plaster to the other face. The edge of the guide board must be in line with the surface of the existing plaster. Carefully lever off the guide board and fill the remaining part of the repair. Wait the required time for the plaster to stiffen before dampening and polishing as described previously. Even though the metal bead is galvanized, take the precaution of painting the corner with a metal primer before decorating. Any cut ends of the bead should be sealed too.

47

# CHAPTER FOUR

# FLOORS

## SIMPLE FLOOR LAYING IN PROBLEM AREAS

In areas where water is often splashed and household cleaners spilt you may wish to lay or renew a floor covering. For speed, ease and low cost, cushioned vinyl could be the answer. This attractive, practical, hard-wearing flooring material only needs to be swept, washed and occasionally polished to keep it in tip-top condition. Cushioned vinyl has a layer of foam material between the surface vinyl and the backing. It is very warm and most comfortable underfoot in a kitchen where much time is spent standing. A layer of glass-fibre gives added strength and stability to the product but does not affect its flexibility. Importantly, it does minimize expansion and contraction. Another advantage is that vinyl floor coverings are good sound and thermal insulators. Provided that all seams are sealed, the whole area becomes impervious to water. Any spillage of acids, alkalis or grease will not affect the surface so long as they are dealt with immediately.

Sheet vinyl is available in a variety of colours to match your own colour scheme. Patterns and effects such as tiles, natural stone and cork are available with surfaces both smooth and textured.

When estimating the amount needed, take into account that vinyl comes in widths of 2, 3 and 4 metres. The wider ones are more difficult to handle without assistance but offer the advantage of needing fewer joins. It's worth making a scale drawing of your floor area. From your sketch you can calculate exactly the area of the room, the amount of vinyl to buy and the most appropriate width. Take into account joins and matching patterns in rooms that are irregular in shape. If you've chosen a repeating pattern, allow for an extra repeat on each length that you order. It's a good idea to take your floor plan to the supplier who will usually give a free estimate on the quantity needed.

## PREPARING YOUR FLOOR

Whatever room you choose to lay vinyl in, there are always DIY methods of ensuring that the surface is well prepared before the vinyl is laid. The prepared surface must be smooth, level, dry, dust- and polish-free and, most importantly, of sound construction. The methods that I describe to prepare the floor and to lay the vinyl floor covering will address the common problems encountered in most floor constructions. Manufacturers produce a leaflet giving basic details of their own products.

### Solid concrete floors

Solid concrete floors should be protected from rising damp by a damp proof membrane. If yours is not, now is a good time to install an inexpensive, easy-to-apply but effective membrane. Three coats of a proprietary brand of bitumen compound are then painted on, following the manufacturer's instructions. First of all check the floor level and check for bumps and hollows. The floor might need a levelling-compound which should be allowed to harden. Your only problem might be that the surface of the concrete is powdery. This is easily solved: a sealer is available and is simply painted on.

If your solid floor already has a damp proof membrane incorporated in the construction you can now fix sheets of good quality plyboard or oil-tempered hardboard to the floor. Drill, plug and screw, but take care not to drill through the membrane. Use alloy or non-rust screws. You can lay vinyl directly on to a concrete floor as long as proper preparation has been made.

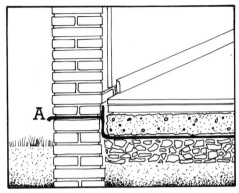

A typical solid concrete floor construction showing the damp proof membrane (**A**) continued up the wall to overlap the damp proof course laid 6in (15cm) above the outside ground level. Under the 4in (10cm) of concrete is 4in (10cm) of compacted hardcore on which is spread sand before the membrane is laid. Above the concrete is 2in (5cm) of mortar screed to support the finished floor.

### Timber floors

To prepare a timber floor is just as easy. Ventilation is essential underneath the wooden floor, so check that the air bricks are not blocked up. If you don't know where cables and pipes are located use a metal detector (cable and pipe finder) and mark on the floor boards with a felt pen. Screw down all loose floor boards and use a nail punch on protruding nail heads. Clean the floor of blobs of plaster and paint. Fill any gaps and plane down high spots. Now cover with ply or oil-tempered hardboard. This hardboard is specially formulated for floors, but lay the smooth side down and use serrated hardboard nails at 4in (10cm) intervals.

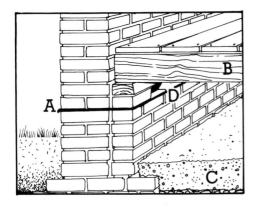

Typical construction of a suspended timber floor showing damp proof course (**A**) 6in (15cm) above ground level and extending in on to the sleeper wall which supports the joists (**B**) on a timber wall plate. The 6in (15cm) of concrete (**C**) is laid on a bed of compacted hardcore. The airbrick (**D**) allows circulation of vented air under the timber floor. Vents are also built into intermediate sleeper walls.

Hardboard should be dampened before fixing and allowed to lay for one day.

Manufacturer's instructions recommend that you do not lay vinyl over a timber floor that has been treated with a wood preservative. There is a DIY method of overcoming this problem. A special product has been manufactured which is simply paper with an aluminium facing, which is laid down to the floor surface. Lay this underneath the plywood or hardboard, whose joints must not coincide with joints in the floor boards. Finally, check that you have a level surface with no screws or nail heads protruding.

## LAYING THE VINYL

Vinyl should be delivered to your home at least 48 hours before you intend to lay it. Slacken the roll and leave it in a warm room so that it will soften and become more pliable. Some manufacturers suggest that you loosely reverse-roll the vinyl or lay it flat. Meantime, you can be cutting your paper pattern! This is the best and surest method of getting an excellent fit right round the room, especially in awkward areas. Making a cutting guide is simplicity itself. It proves itself when laying vinyl in a bathroom, where a professional finish around a hand basin or WC pedestal is essential. Felt paper used as carpet underlay is inexpensive to buy from a large roll and is ideal for making a cutting pattern. It comes in large pieces, it can be left under the vinyl, it will soften any small defects in the floor and, it will add to the life of the vinyl and give a superior finish to the floor covering.

Follow these simple stages to make the paper pattern:

1  Cover the floor with the felt paper
2  Tape the joins
3  Cut the paper to within 2in (50mm) of all edges
4  Fix the paper to the floor with tape or drawing pins
5  Draw an outline of the room on the paper by running a small block of wood with a felt pen firmly taped to it all around the walls, pipes, pedestals and freestanding objects. Keep checking that the felt pen has not moved
6  Remove the felt carefully in one piece

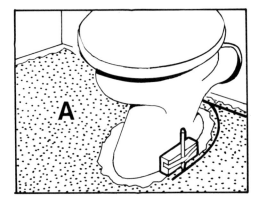

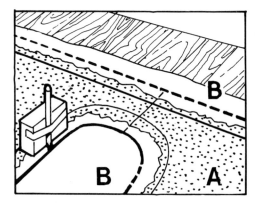

Cover and temporarily fix a sheet of felt paper (**A**) over the whole of the room cutting it short of the walls and obstacles. By running a block and felt pen against skirting boards and obstacles you mark an outline on the felt-paper template. Keep the block of wood at exactly 90° to each surface to obtain an exact replica of the room but smaller by the size of the block.

In a larger room lay down the vinyl. Carefully lay the felt-paper template (**A**) flat on to the vinyl sheet (**B**) and with the block now against the drawn outline reverse the drawing order by making an exact copy of the shape of the room on the vinyl (**B**). Cut with a sharp trimming knife. Holes in the sheet vinyl for a lavatory will need a slit from the hole to the back edge.

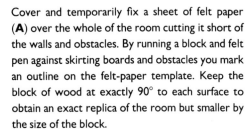

You'll now need a flat area larger than the area of the vinyl to be cut. The following step-by-step instructions will ensure that your vinyl flooring fits perfectly everywhere:

I  Lay the vinyl face up. If the room to be covered is too large for a single piece off the roll, tape pieces together matching the pattern

2  Place the felt-paper template on top and tape it carefully (without creases or movement) into place

3  Use the same block with the felt pen taped to it, to mark a new line on the vinyl, holding the wooden block this time against the scribed line on the felt paper

5  Slowly and carefully cut the vinyl,

following the line, using a straight edge and trimming knife on the straight runs and scissors or a trimming knife on the curves

An alternative to the block and felt pen is to use a pair of compasses with a locking device. Lock the compass at about 2in (50mm) radius and draw a test circle on a piece of card to use as check throughout the tracing procedure. With the point vertically against the wall trace a line on to the felt paper template with a felt pen. Remember that the open compass must be kept at exactly 90° to the wall or fitting to ensure a perfect tracing. For pipes and true circles mark the difference from the pipe with the compass in four positions and form a square. This is easily transferred to the vinyl, mark diagonals across the square giving you the exact centre of the pipe. For freestanding fittings, for example a WC pedestal, a single straight cut in the felt paper behind the fitting will allow you to fit the pattern right round to be taped at the back.

Decide whether you are going to loose-lay or stick down the vinyl. Vinyl can be loose-laid when one piece is used, although you should still stick down the area around the door. The manufacturer will recommend the appropriate adhesive. When laying more than one piece, always stick down the vinyl at the ends and along each seam with adhesive or double-sided sticky tape. Some

manufacturers recommend sticking down the whole of the sheet vinyl covering. Use a notched spreader to apply the adhesive to the floor. Press in the vinyl firmly with a clean, dampened cloth but always wipe off excess with a separate dampened cloth.

When checking the quality of the vinyl, a good tip is to run a thumb nail across the backing layer. It should remain firm and not break up at all. The overall thickness of vinyl is not a true assessment of quality. Some high quality vinyls are denser and longer lasting than thicker ones of a lower standard. If the vinyl is to be laid on a floor with under-floor heating, choose a good quality contract cushioned vinyl. It is available in a wide range of colours and designs.

## FIXING NOISY FLOORS

Floors are generally made up of two elements: the structural or supporting part, and the flooring, which is the boarding or covering laid on to the structural base. The structural element can either be timber floor joists or a concrete slab. (See illustration pp.49–50) In an ordinary house the ground floors can be either solid or suspended, whilst the upper floors are constructed of heavy timber joists supported either end in the walls. Before the turn of the century most ground floors of modest houses were built of suspended timber floor construction. Early in the twentieth century designers began to appreciate the merits of solid floor construction. The concrete slab was laid on a 6in (15cm) bed of compacted rubble or hard core, its top surface waterproofed with asphalt. Any one of a number of floor finishes could then be laid – floorboards on

joists, tiles in a bed of screed, or a sand and cement screed for a covering of sheet material. By the late 1920s to early 1930s, solid concrete floor construction had generally superseded the timber ground floor in houses in this country.

To check whether a ground floor is solid or of a suspended timber floor construction, just walk outside and look for tell-tale air bricks. It is essential that the air space between the floor joists and the ground level in a suspended timber floor construction is ventilated, to prevent damp and conditions conducive to rot.

Previously, joists of upper floors were supported half-way, on a long span, by a load-bearing wall. Otherwise they were designed to be laid to bridge the shortest span. Where joists had no intermediate support, a heavier joist would be used and often braced with solid strutting. Criss-cross or herring-bone bracing gave extra rigidity to the joists. Nowadays, proprietary metal herringbone strutting is available. Without bracing or strutting – an integral part of upper-floor construction – joists can warp and twist, and this is often the cause of cracks in ceilings as well as movement in flooring. Any movement between boards or between boards and joists will eventually give rise to creaking sounds. The nail holes enlarge, the floor nails loose their hold and the floorboards rock and creak.

Floor nails or brads can loose their hold for other reasons. Rot or an attack of woodworm in the joists will cause the timber to crumble. Shrinkage in the actual floorboards can cause movement and creaks. Warping and bowing can be caused by central heating pipes being too hot or too close to the floorboards. Floorboards not properly fixed or rocking on bent or rusted floor brads will cause the squeaky noise.

When faced with the problem of creaking floorboards always observe this golden rule: never try to nail back a board before first lifting it to make an inspection. Underneath most floors can be found one or all of the following: electric cables, television or telephone cables, domestic water pipes, central heating pipes and gas pipes. If any of these services run parallel to the joists, it is easy for the builder to isolate them from floor-fixing nails or screws, but if they run at right angles to the joists they must be directed through the centres of the joists. Unfortunately, it is sometimes necessary to cut notches in the tops of the joists for the services, making them very vulnerable to floor fixings. Ordinary floorboards are fixed by nailing or screwing near the edges of each board into each joist. Notches are cut and pipes laid along the centres of floorboards. Add to your house information folder a plan of each floor showing all the services as you go through the problem solving work.

If you see the tell-tale flight-holes of woodworm, treat the joists and the surrounding timbers with a proprietary woodworm fluid. If necessary strengthen the floor joist by bolting a piece of timber alongside it. Rotted or broken floorboards must be replaced.

## REPLACING DAMAGED FLOORBOARDS

If a floorboard is badly split or part of it needs to be replaced, cut out the part to be replaced centrally over joists. If the replacement board is of a different thickness you can do one of two things. If the only new board available is thinner, use packing pieces of hardboard or ply nailed to the joists. Should the new board be slightly thicker than the existing cut grooves in the underside surface to coincide with the joists.

Take great care when prising up a floorboard not to split it. Sometimes floor brads are left behind rusted in the joists. Remove them with a claw hammer and punch below the surface of the joists any snapped-off ends. A floorboard with a twist will sometimes refuse to flatten if nails are used, brass or alloy screws are best used in this case.

Sometimes it is necessary to re-fix all the floorboards in a room. Should this or the

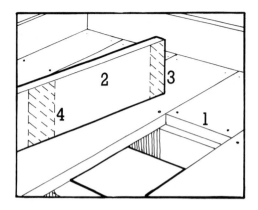 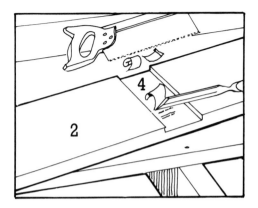

When part of a floorboard has to be replaced, make the cut half-way over a joist (1). Mark the new board (2) if it is too thick, ready for chiselling as at (3) and (4).

Cut parallel lines, slightly wider than the width of the joist, with a tenon saw. Use a bevel-edged chisel to remove the waste wood (4) so that the thickness of the board left will bring the floorboard level with the existing. Turn the board (2) over and fix as for normal boards.

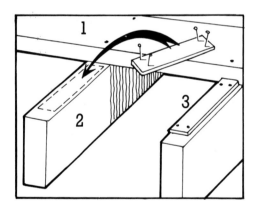

If the replacement board is slightly thinner than the existing boards simply cut and fix packing pieces of hardboard or plywood (3) so that the board can be brought level with the adjacent floorboards (1). Glue the pieces in place and use 1 in (25mm) panel pins for fixing to the joists (2).

replacing of floorboards be necessary, take the opportunity to check all the joists. The ends particularly are vulnerable to damp and rot. All joists will benefit from an extra application of preservative. If a joist has to be replaced now is the time to do it. A floor that shows signs of bounce near a wall could have a spongy end to a joist. If this is the case, cut off the rotted end and bolt a galvanized bower beam to the end of the joist. Check for spaces between the undersides of joists and supporting walls or small sleeper walls at ground floor level. If there is a space the floor will give when walked on and this movement can produce creaks. To solve this simply pack small pieces of slate between the sleeper wall and the joist. When laying floorboards use hired floor cramps which effectively push the boards tightly together before nailing.

If a floor at ground level has to be replaced, take the opportunity to install under-floor insulation. Staple a lightweight polythene net between the timbers, slackly enough to allow glass-fibre insulation to be rolled out so that it fits tightly between the joists.

Part of the construction of a solid concrete ground floor is the damp proof membrane. This barrier to moisture is essential to keep floor coverings dry. Joists laid on a solid floor to support timber flooring need ventilation too to keep them in good condition. Even though joists are supported along the whole of their length, timber still moves. A joist can bow upwards producing bounce, movement and creaks when walked on. Floorboards can suffer the same problems as when used on a suspended floor construction: shrinkage, creaking and loose nails producing movement and wear.

### Tongue and grooved floorboards

Chipboard decking is used often as flooring over a solid ground floor. The sheets are usually long, narrow and tongue and grooved. The last one laid will have the underside of the groove cut away for easy fixing, which in turn makes it easy for that one to be prised off especially if it was fixed with nails. Special alloy screws should always be used to fix chipboard flooring; and if you haven't used a cordless screwdriver, try one. They're inexpensive and turn a chore into a joy! Imagine half a day's work driving in screws the traditional tedious and tiring way. With the use of this brilliant tool,

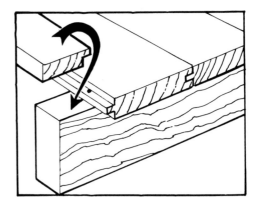

The traditional square-edged floorboard has a number of drawbacks. Gaps are left when they shrink, they curl and nails are loosened as they shrink. Tongue and groove or 'T&G' boards have a tongue running centrally along the one edge and a matching groove along the other. This makes for a strong joint. Fixing is by 'secret nailing' through the tongue into the joist. At the skirting, cut the board to width and cut off the lower section of the groove.

no effort is needed and it takes only a quarter of the time.

Tongue and grooved floorboards can creak for no apparent reason. The tongue is very thin and runs the whole length of the board and should fit tightly into the groove. The slightest shrinkage in the boards allows the delicate strips of wood to rub against each other. If the problem is only slight, solve it by dusting talcum powder into the joints. You can find out if you've got tongue and groove boards by inserting a thin blade between the boards. The first board is the trickiest to remove, the rest are easy to prise up with a couple of chisels. In order to lift the first board, cut through the tongue with a flooring saw or a pad saw held at a shallow angle. Beware of cables and pipes and as a precaution turn off the main services. For refixing in problem areas always use screws. The advantages are firmer and longer holding and easy removal at problem times.

## Skirting board

The last board to be fixed in the construction of a suspended timber floor is the skirting board. Removing the end of a board that is tucked underneath the skirting board is quite easy. Cut the floorboard centrally over a joist with a flooring saw, or at the side of the joist with a pad saw, held at an angle (with your hand over the joist). A 2in × 1in (5cm × 2.5cm) batten nailed to the side of the joist will support the replacement board. Prise the board up from the joist until the board is free on the last joist which should always be located a few inches from the wall. You'll see the end of the floorboard dip down between the last joist and the bottom of the skirting board which allows it to be withdrawn very simply. For safety's sake always remove nails from boards and joists immediately they are exposed. To lift a square-edged floorboard insert a chisel or lever into a convenient end and prise up. If it's a tight fit, hammer it in but take great care. Insert a second lever further along, moving each one and levering until the board is free. Another method is to pop a tube or rod under the eased board and press down the free end with your foot. Continue to roll the rod along under the board as the nails are lifted.

If a number of boards have to be lifted

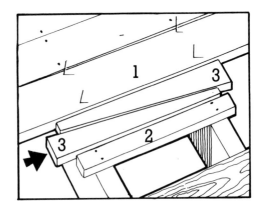

The next floorboard to be fixed (**1**) can be forced into position to make a tight fit by using folding wedges (**3**). Nail a batten (**2**) to the joists first as a temporary support for the wedges. Slide the wedges (cut diagonally from a spare board) into position. Hammer the wedges as indicated at the arrow to get a tight fit before securing the floorboard with nails into each joist.

and replaced, use folding-wedges, a DIY method of tightening the boards to each other, if a flooring-cramp is not available. Folding wedges are made from a spare piece of square-edged board about 2ft (50cm) long. Cut the board diagonally lengthways. Lay the wedges in position against the last loose board and slide them apart about 8in (20cm). Nail a temporary batten support against the folding wedges. By hammering the wedges together you get an extremely tight fit between the floorboards. Always brush the undersides of the boards and the tops of joists before fixing to ensure that no debris is going to cause creaking problems in the future.

## UPGRADING A WORN WOODEN FLOOR

Technical developments in the building industry have contributed to the need for less maintenance in our homes. UPVC windows, for example, once installed are maintenance-free for life. Roof, ceiling, wall and floor coverings are all available in durable man-made materials, and over the past decade there has been an upsurge in the interest and use of them. However, there are still people for whom there is no substitute for natural materials. The 'disenchanted' is joining the 'traditionalist' in his great love of the beauty, texture and warmth of natural materials in the home. There is no substitute for a smooth, highly-polished oak, beech or pine floor, with a sparkling finish to highlight the beauty of the grain. Obtaining this high-quality floor finish is no longer a job for

professionals only as all the necessary tools can now be hired. All you need is the patience and tenacity to see the job through. It is a time-consuming one, and the machines make a lot of noise and dust. A vacuum-bag is incorporated in the drum-sander, but you still need to use protective clothing, a nose-mask and even perhaps goggles.

There has been a tremendous growth in the DIY hire shop business and it costs relatively little to hire an expensive piece of equipment or tool for a weekend's DIY job. By hiring an industrial sanding machine, a rotary sander and a hook scraper, it is possible in just one weekend to change a scratched, discoloured and neglected floor into a smooth, flat, sanded one.

## PREPARATION

Preparation, as in all DIY jobs, is very important. After the room has been emptied of furniture and floor coverings, thoroughly vacuum the floor so that all blemishes and any worm holes will be exposed. If there is woodworm infestation, lift the board that is worst affected. The back of the board might show even more holes, which will mean that there's a honeycomb of larvae tunnels inside the wood. Examine the adjacent boards and burn those that have more than just a few holes. Treat all the surrounding timber before laying the new matching floorboards. Boards that show any signs of rot must be burned and replaced. Some boards might be split where they've been cut and lifted by someone laying cables or central heating pipes. In most towns either an architectural

reclamation yard or a demolition yard selling second-hand timber can be found. Otherwise use new replacement timber but stain it to match the existing boards.

For a professional finish to your floor, there should be no gaps. It is not too difficult to lift boards and to re-lay them tightly butted together. The last gap left next to the skirting board must be filled with a new board. Re-laying the floor provides a good opportunity to thermally insulate it, too. (*See* pp.105–6.)

Every nail holding down a board must be punched at least $\frac{1}{8}$in (3mm) below the surface. Screws must be driven in to the same depth. The abrasive paper attached to the spinning sanding drum will be torn to shreds if one small tack is left! Check very

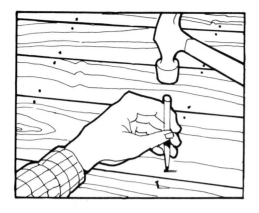

Before using the sanding machine check the entire floor for signs of worm holes and treat as neces-

sary. A raised head of a floor brad (nail) will rip the abrasive paper of the sanding machine, so be certain that every suspect nail is driven below the surface with a nail punch. A proprietary wood filler can fill the nail holes – use one that matches the floor colour.

carefully at the same time for loose boards, especially where a cut board has been re-laid over a joist. Plane a piece of lath to fit tightly into any odd gap between boards. Apply a wood adhesive and hammer it home. Use a smoothing plane to level it, and stain it if necessary.

## LEVELLING AN UNEVEN FLOOR

Most old floors, especially those made of standard pine boards, are likely to have

Very few floors are absolutely flat. To solve this problem sand diagonally one way and then the other way. Then sand parallel to the boards with a medium grade sanding paper to give a smooth finish and to sand out any scratches.

uneven surfaces across the width of some of the boards. An inward curve, called cupping, is the most common and obvious. Before even thinking about the final smooth finish, it is necessary to level the floor. Full instructions come with the hired machines and now is the time to read and re-read them in order to make no mistakes! A new sheet of abrasive paper, you will note, must be fitted only after unplugging the lead from the electric socket. Make sure that the sanding sheet is wrapped tightly around the drum and aligned properly. The paper can be torn to shreds if it is not secure. The information leaflet will also suggest sealing around openings with masking tape. Fine dust is drawn very easily through gaps around and underneath doors. One window, however, can be left open to provide fresh air. Now make sure that the machine is switched off before plugging back into the mains.

Often it is very useful to know a trades-man's method of carrying out a job, especially where a little special knowledge is required. No one serves an apprenticeship in floor sanding, but a carpenter knows that planing or sanding diagonally across a piece of wood will level it! That is why the professional sands diagonally over the whole area of the floor one way and then diagonally the other way. Do this and you'll end up with a perfectly level floor, with no cupping across any of the floorboards. Use the rotary edging sander to work close to skirting boards. A small orbital sander or a hook scraper will clean up the corners. Three or four grades of abrasive paper are normally used, working progressively from the coarse to begin with down to a fine grade to obtain the smoothest possible finish. Remember always to unplug from the socket before making any change or adjustment to an electrically-operated machine.

An upright drum sander is quite heavy and very powerful. It can exert a strong pull, so take care not to let it run away. With the cable looped over your shoulder, hold the sander very securely, tilt it back and switch it on. When it's up to speed, lower the drum gently to the floor and allow it to move forward. Try not to be hesitant, walk slowly and steadily as it moves forward under its own power. Only hold the machine to control its pace forward, never ever leave it stationary. Holding a rotating drum in the same spot for even a moment will cause gouging. When you reach the end of one line, push the handle down to lift the drum off the floor. Switch off and wait for the drum to stop revolving before starting the reverse line. Use a vacuum cleaner as often

as is necessary to remove the residual dust.

The next part of the operation could cause knee problems, so get yourself some soft kneeling pads! This is the best position for using the edging sander. It is not a difficult machine to use because it generates its own gliding action and has back castor wheels to lift the disc off the floor. Make sure that the electric cable is over your shoulder before switching on and lowering the machine. Again, it is essential to keep the machine moving. No pressure has to be exerted on the machine but it is essential to keep the machine moving in all directions. Always tilt the machine back on to its castors before switching off. Each time you change the abrasive disc, remember to pull the plug from the socket first.

There will be areas of the floor that cannot be reached by the floor sander or the rotary sander which is used on long runs against skirting boards. Use a hook scraper — a long handled, simple-to-use tool which cuts as it is pulled backwards. Blades are interchangeable and can get into tight corners.

After levelling the floor with the coarse-grade paper, change to a medium-grade to sand in the same direction as the boards. Never ever sand at right angles to the boards. Overlap each line so that there are no misses. Don't forget to use the same grade of abrasive paper each time on the rotary sander too. Continue to use the vacuum cleaner to remove spillage and excess dust and to prevent too much dust rising into the room. Progress to the finest of the abrasive sheets until you are satisfied you've attained a smooth satin finish. After vacuuming the floor use a clean cloth and white spirit to remove all traces of dust. Now is the time to go outside and shake out all your working clothes; you'll be surprised by the amount of dust stuck in clumps to the bottom of your shoes. Every trace must be removed including from the tops of skirting boards, before the sealing treatment is started.

## SEALING

Left untreated at this stage, the floor quickly picks up dirt, is hard to clean, becomes stained and less resistant to wear. Sealing a sanded wooden floor must be tackled as quickly as possible. A clear-finish sealing treatment not only creates an attractive feature, but is necessary to preserve, seal and protect the floor.

The principle of a satisfactory seal is that it should penetrate a little below the surface and also coat the surface. The final coat, of two or three applications, needs to be hard-wearing, attractive-looking, easily-maintained and readily-renewed in due course.

Many of the modern sealing products meet these criteria. Some people find solvent-based finishes inappropriate because of the smell. In this case, try a water-borne varnish, which is very quick-drying: touch-dry in 20 minutes and hard enough to be recoatable in two hours. Whichever you use, always follow the manufacturer's instructions and recommended times between coats. Always lightly rub down with very fine glass paper in between coats but do make sure that the seal is hard and dry first, and always remove dust with a clean cloth and white spirit.

## REPLACING A WOODEN FLOOR WITH A SOLID FLOOR

Pre-twentieth-century ground floor construction in speculative building was often of poor quality. The subfloor constructions and sleeper walls were found to be built on brick rubble. Poor ventilation encouraged dry rot and the air space below the boards provided a source of cold air through gaps to the room above. When it was discovered that older buildings were suffering rot and woodworm in ground floor timbers, the principles of ground floor construction were improved. It was cheaper, easier and more convenient to lay a solid floor of concrete. This also solved the problem of draughts.

Solid floors are now the norm for builders and DIYers except that the job is made easier by being able to order the exact amount of ready-mixed concrete to be delivered!

## PREPARATION

Remove every trace of timber; burn rotten or damaged timbers but keep and treat the rest with preservative. Clean and store the skirting boards and the doors. Pull nails through from the back of a skirting board or saw them off flush to the timber. Trying to knock them through the front face of the board will result in long splits and ugly holes. Now check the air vents. Often one floor void will

be the only source of ventilation to another. If this is the case, make certain that you can provide through ventilation by adding an extra air brick. Treat the ground and surrounding brickwork with a fungicide and repair the perimeter interior walls. The sleeper walls will contribute to the hard core base.

## LAYING THE FLOOR

Now check and mark the level of the existing damp proof course in the walls. It is essential that the damp proof membrane, which is a sheet of 1200 gauge polythene, links up with or overlaps the damp proof course in the adjoining walls. The next stage is to mark a series of chalk lines around the four walls to which must be levelled the various layers making up the solid floor. This is one way of discovering how much you have to excavate, if the void is too shallow, fill in, if it is too deep. The first layer is of rubble or broken bricks to a minimum depth of 4in (100mm). Up to 20in (510mm) of hard core can be safely laid without fear of settlement. However, each third of that depth should be very well compacted with a hired plate vibrator. The next layer is the blinding of sand, to cover all the crevices and sharp edges. Make certain that there are no sharp points otherwise the polythene membrane which is laid on the blinding could be punctured and allow damp through. Turn up the edges of the membrane to overlap the DPM in the walls. Any joints in the membrane must overlap by 10in (250mm) and be sealed

against moisture penetration with a proprietary waterproof tape.

Concrete is a mixture of cement, sharp sand, aggregate, which is either crushed stone or gravel, and water. The exact amounts of each of the parts is very important in the mix. Too much water should not be used or it will weaken the concrete and cause shrinking when it dries. The mix for this purpose should be 1 part cement to 2½ parts sharp sand and 4 parts aggregate. Hire a concrete-mixer or order direct from a ready-mix company. A few telephone calls to establish costs will help you make up your mind.

You'll need to wear work clothes, gloves and wellington boots for the next part of the job. Very few tools are needed: a straight long length of 4in×2in (100mm × 50mm) timber for tamping the concrete and a spirit level for checking the surface level with the chalk line. Starting at the furthest point from the door, lay long narrow bands of concrete the width of the room (about 20in (510mm) wide). The concrete will set firmly enough over 24 hours for boards to be laid to walk on. Then find yourself another DIY job to do for four days! Sprinkle water on the surface at least once a day and cover it over to slow down the curing process. Then there's no chance of shrinkage.

After a week, or a minimum of four days, the screed can be laid. This is a finer mix of 3 parts sharp sand to 1 part cement. It is fairly easy to lay and a most satisfying job to accomplish. Before laying the screed the

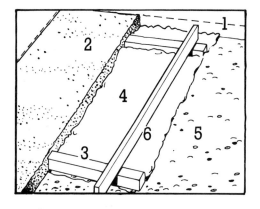

The dotted line (**1**) is the finished level of the top of the screed (**2**) already laid in the first bay. Battens (**3**), of the same thickness as the screed, are laid in mortar. A cement grout (**4**) is laid between the battens on the concrete floor (**5**). The screed is laid between and either side of the battens and levelled with the tamping batten (**6**). Lift out the battens and fill in with screed material.

concrete floor needs to be primed. Mix a slurry of cement, water and a bonding agent. As with the concrete, work in bands from one end of the room back towards the door. Brush on a covering of slurry to cover the area of the first band and just in from each wall lay a level batten into mortar. Level the battens to the chalk line indicating the screed surface. Shovel the screed mortar along the band between the battens and level it with the tamping batten laid across the two battens. Finish either side of the battens and smooth the surface with a wooden float. Immediately, you can lift out the battens and fill the hollows, carefully levelling them with the float. Each of the subsequent bands undergoes exactly the same procedure. You should have 3 to 4in (75 to 100mm) of polythene membrane showing right round the room tight to the walls. The screed also needs at least a week to cure. Now it's the waiting period. It will take three or four months to cure and dry out completely. Trim the polythene membrane 1 to 2in (25 to 50mm) above the screed. The re-fixed skirting board will hold it in position. The top of the screed will have finished at exactly the right depth below the door opening to accommodate your chosen floor covering which could be 1in (25mm) of oak or beech strip flooring, ¾in (20mm) of underlay and carpet or ⅜in (10mm) of oil tempered hardboard and cork or vinyl tiles.

## FIXING CREAKY STAIRS

Most households suffer from the 'familiarity' syndrome! A tiny scuff mark on the bottom of a door is hardly noticeable. A little grease spot near a light switch is easily overlooked.

A creak in a stairtread registers only momentarily. These unwanted sights and sounds around our homes become part of our lives; subconsciously they become

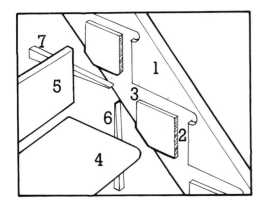

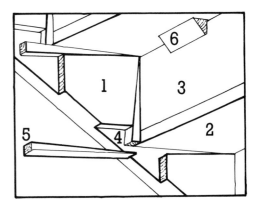

The two main side supports of a stairs, the 'strings' (1), have matching grooves cut into them. The vertical ones (2) take the 'risers' (5) and the horizontal the tread (4). The grooves are tapered so that a wedge (6) is hammered in behind the riser and another one (7) underneath the tread to ensure a tight fit with no creaks!

The component parts of the stairs seen from underneath. The string (1) with the tread (2) and riser (3) in position. The vertical wedge (4) trimmed so that the horizontal wedge (5) can be hammered into place. Two glue blocks (6) are fixed into the angle between the tread and riser. If any are missing creaks will result. Cut them diagonally from 2 × 2in (50 × 50mm) softwood about 6in (150mm) long.

familiar and we accept them. But the inevitable happens – paint falls off the door, grease marks spread, holding dirt and grime, and the creaking stairs become a noticeable bounce.

We can enjoy far more comfort and suffer much less worry in our homes by having a positive attitude to what appear to be irritating but significant repair jobs. It's so easy to say, 'I'll do it later'! The inconvenience tends to put us off the minor jobs, coupled with the fear of the unknown, not knowing the correct solvent to clean grease off wallpaper, how to repair chipped paint, or whether you'll need a carpenter to rebuild part of the staircase. To put things right is often a very simple matter indeed and 'to put things right' could not be more apt or

simple when confronted with the problem of creaking stairs.

A good staircase is the result of the carpenter's skill at measuring, cutting and fitting together component parts with great precision. It is not an elaborate or complicated piece of joinery. Stairs are formed from three basic elements – treads, risers and stringers. However, these are the parts that suffer most from constant wear. It is helpful to know how they are constructed, so that repairs can be carried out whenever creaks and gaps begin to appear.

Stairs have two main side supports called stringers or strings. The top edge of a closed string is parallel to the lower edge, but an open string staircase has the string cut to the shape of the steps. Each step of an ordinary straight flight is made from two boards, the horizontal tread and the vertical riser which forms the front of the step. The riser is fixed underneath the nosing or front edge of one tread and the back edge of another. The strings have a matching series of vertical and horizontal grooves cut into them. The risers and treads are glued into these tapered grooves and are held in position with long thin wedges of hardwood. The wedges are driven in to ensure a tight fit with no creaks.

Joints between treads and risers can be made in a number of ways, and small triangular glue blocks are fixed into the joint underneath the stairs. Now check the illustrations to see exactly how the component parts are assembled. With this knowledge and information it is easy to appreciate that creaks in stairs begin only when joints become loose and start rubbing. Shrinking timber can also contribute to the slight gaps that allow movement and creaks. So to solve the problem, a carpenter is not needed nor is expertise at joinery. It really is simply a matter of refitting, glueing and screwing.

## LOCATING CREAKS

If the exact location of the creak is obvious and the underside of the stairs is accessible and not boarded over, this is where the best and easiest repair can be made. Should the underside of the stairs be boarded over, it is possible to solve the problem effectively from above, but to locate the problem from

below, you will need help. A child will do but preferably a big one! Their simple contribution is to walk up and down the stairs a couple of times while you locate the exact position of gaps and creaks. From underneath the stairs mark each tread and riser and mark where creaks occur.

## PROBLEM AREAS

If the edge of a tread or a riser is loose in its groove, you'll find that the wedge will need re-fitting. Prise out the original wedge carefully and clean it up with medium grade glass paper. If the wedge is missing or damaged it's a very simple job to make a new one. Usually the wedge to the riser is put in first sawn off flush with the underside of the tread and then a longer wedge is driven in underneath the tread. Should you have to remove or replace a wedge to a riser, you might have to loosen or lift out the longer wedge first. Very little skill is needed to apply wood glue and to re-wedge the joint.

Use a claw hammer and a spare piece of timber to protect the end grain of the wedge. Don't be tempted to use nails as the wedges will easily split especially if they are hardwood. Your assistant can now do the test bounce! By shifting weight to and fro above the replaced wedge, check that that part of the staircase is cured of creaks.

General wear and tear of this much abused functional link between one floor and another contributes to the problem of loose or missing glue blocks. Normally two blocks are fixed to each joint between riser and tread. A loose or missing block is likely to be one of the locations for a creak. It is possible for glue to fail on just one face and the block to remain in position. This will also give rise to a creak. Original blocks fixed by the joiner are never nailed so it should not split when you carefully prise it off. The smallest nib of old wood glue left on the block will prevent flush contact when it is replaced. Use a medium glass paper to thoroughly clean all surfaces.

A DIY tip to ensure a better result! With a long screwdriver, gently prise open the joint between the tread and riser to be able to apply the wood adhesive there. Drill a pilot hole at an angle to be able to pull the joint together with a screw. Use a 1½in (38mm) countersink screw and make sure the head is set below the surface of the riser. After applying glue to both surfaces of the block, slide it back and forth three or four times whilst pushing it home. This will get rid of bubbles and ensure perfect contact and adhesion. Small panel pins can be used while the adhesive sets and then removed. Leave a note on the stair above the repair so that the wood glue has time to set properly!

If missing blocks cannot be found amongst the storage under the stairs, new ones can easily be cut from 2in × 2in (50mm × 50mm) soft wood. By setting a piece of timber upright in a vice and sawing down diagonally – about 6in (150mm) – four blocks can be made, each 3in (76mm) long. Reposition the timber horizontally, cut accurately across the grain and there you have your new glue blocks.

Having dealt with the internal angle between tread and riser, now check the external angle. The joint here is very vulnerable to opening because the underside of it has no solid support. The pounding to which the back of the tread is subjected only compounds the problem. Fortunately, solving it is comparatively simple. Prise open the joint slightly, to inject adhesive into it, and use screws to pull and hold the joint together. Check the thickness of the timbers before deciding whether to use a No. 6 or No. 8 screw. Countersink screw heads beneath the surface of the wood. Some modern staircases incorporate a ply riser. If the section of ply is too thin to hold a screw successfully, there is a simple alternative. Cut a piece of ⅜in (10mm) ply about 2ft (½ metre) long. Glue and screw this to the back edge of the tread and to the riser. If the position is convenient and you can manoeuvre a prop into position, wedge a length of timber between that tread and the floor. This will ensure a tight, close joint while the wood glue is setting.

Working from above the stairs is actually simpler but you have the carpet to contend with first! If spiked gripper strips have been used and the carpet laid by a professional, he will have started at the bottom of the staircase. Gripper strip is fixed to the back of the tread and the bottom of the riser. The carpet is pushed into this joint with a tool similar to a bolster chisel and held securely. To remove it you simply jerk it free. On winding stairs the excess from the tread is tucked behind the carpet covering the riser. At the top of the stairs the carpet is nailed against the riser on the last tread and the landing carpet brought over the top step to meet it. By reversing the process you can then unroll the carpet down the stairs as far as you need to carry out your creaking stair repair.

Working from above the stairs means that you can dispense with the services of your assistant! You can better identify the problem by shifting your weight back and forth on any part of the stair that is moving and creaking. To solve the problem of creaking in the joint underneath the nosing of the tread you just need to use screws to pull the joint together. Notice that the nosing overhangs the riser, which makes accurate measuring essential, so that the screw centres on the riser itself. After having drilled countersunk pilot holes, inject wood glue into them. This is the method by which glue is spread into the wooden joint around the screw.

If the stairs are uncovered polished wood, there is a DIY method of covering the screw heads and producing a professional finish. Change the bit in your power drill to a plug cutter bit and use matching timber. The plug cutter will be the same diameter as the countersunk hole which of course must be drilled slightly deeper. Making plugs is satisfying because, instead of drilling holes, the bit actually drills and brings out perfect small plugs. Ten can be produced in as many seconds! These plugs are then glued into countersunk screw holes to cover the screw heads. Use a fine grade sanding block to obtain a smooth finish.

If the problem is looseness at the point where the tread or riser meets the string, it is possible to drive screws in at an angle. The bit making your pilot hole should emerge at the bottom edge of the tread. Use a 2in (50mm) No. 8 screw countersunk.

The joint at the back of the tread is the final one to be tackled. If the staircase is carpeted, glue and pin a long length of triangular moulding between the horizontal and vertical gripper strips. Try also to prise open the joint to inject wood glue as deeply as possible. Of necessity, the moulding will have to be a small section otherwise the gripper will not get adequate hold. If, on the other hand, the staircase is uncarpeted a larger section of matching wood can be glued and screwed in the joint between the riser and tread. A matching wood filler will cover the countersunk screw heads. The construction of staircases is subject to stringent building regulation specifications. The only one that is of any concern here is the 8¾in (222mm) measured back from the nosing of a tread to a mark vertically below the nosing of the next highest tread.

# CHAPTER FIVE

# WALLS
# AND
# CEILINGS

## PANELLING UNEVEN WALLS

Often an inside wall in an older house that has been giving problems over the years will have cracks and patches showing in the plaster. Of the 20 million home owners in this country there must be hundreds of thousands with the problem of not quite knowing what to do with uneven walls. Neither painting nor wallpapering can disguise bumps and hollows. There is, however, a popular and simple remedy that literally transforms the look of a room. If, like me, you love the beauty inherent in the grain of natural wood, then use natural timber wall cladding. It will enhance the appearance and atmosphere of any room. It is not difficult to install, adds extra insulation and overcomes any problems of condensation on that particular wall.

In simple terms pre-treated battens are fixed to the wall, then tongue and groove boarding is 'secret-nailed' to them. What you are effectively doing is designing a framework on to which the cladding will be fixed. Buy pre-treated softwood for the framework. An external wall will need a vapour barrier of polythene sheeting stapled

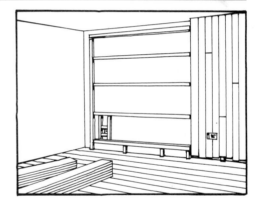

Before fixing treated battens to an exterior wall use a sheet of polythene tacked to the wall to prevent condensation. Remove skirting boards, picture rails and coving and be prepared to bring forward switch and socket covers. Construct a framework of battens to which the cut ends around the sockets are fixed. To prevent splitting the ends of the panelling boards keep the wall battens in from corners and ceiling. Fix short 'grounds' to which the skirting boards are refixed. Always switch off at the mains or remove fuse before unscrewing socket covers.

or pinned to it. A full wall being cladded will need to have skirting boards removed. Check for pipes and cables and arrange your battens to miss them. If you need to check for hidden cables use a DIY metal detector (cable and pipe finder). Make a scale drawing of the wall and show the exact positions of cables and pipes. Keep it for future reference. To order the right amount of timber wall cladding, measure the height and the width of the wall to be covered and multiply them to get the surface area. The cladding comes in packs, so it's very easy to buy the correct number – allowing a little extra for waste! Now check these three points. Firstly, if the wall is damp, you must trace the source, effect a cure and let it dry out. (*See* Chapter 2) Secondly, store the timber cladding in the room where it's going to be used. Let it adjust to the temperature and the atmosphere of that room by laying for a few days. Thirdly, take great care with electrics, that is, a switch or a socket outlet. You might have to bring the switch cover plate forward over the cladding but it is simple and safe to do this provided that you have switched off the circuit at the mains first. One further golden rule: all wood panelling must stop short of a heating appliance, boiler or open fire. You can buy metal guards or trims to protect boards that have to be fixed near any source of heat. Always use a non-combustible material to protect the wall cladding in such situations.

Fixing cladding to a stud partition wall is relatively easy because the battens for the framework can be nailed or screwed to the studs and noggings (the horizontal pieces nailed between the upright studs). To find out exactly where the wooden framework is in the partition wall use a stud sensor, a very useful and inexpensive addition to your tool kit.

Fixing cladding to a solid wall usually means drilling, plugging and screwing. The arrangement of the battening is important because you don't want to end up with a wall that gives under the slightest pressure. Battens must not be positioned close to ceilings or corners, otherwise fixing nails will split the ends of the boards. Cladding boards, ½in (12mm) thick, generally need battens placed 20in (510mm) apart. If they are less than ½in (12mm) thick, then fix the battens 16in (400mm) apart. Use a spirit level at all times. The ideal cross-section of the battens should be 1½in × 1in (38mm ×

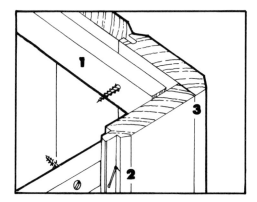

Battens are fixed horizontally (**1**) for vertical cladding. The boards are fixed with the groove sliding on to the tongue of the last fixed board. Nail through the inside corner of the tongue at an angle (**2**). Use a nail punch to hide the nail head below the surface. Remove the tongue from the corner panel and the groove from the adjacent one to join at the corner (**3**).

25mm). These are fixed to the wall horizontally for vertical cladding and vertically for horizontal cladding. Work out by trial and error the positions of battens on your particular wall. Keep them fairly close to switches and sockets but do be careful and take into account the live cables feeding those switches and sockets. (*See* illustration, page 00) A plastic switch box held to a stud position wall by two 'flick over' arms is simplicity itself to bring forward on to your cladding. Check though that there is sufficient cable first. Should you need to bring the mounting box forward, remove the two fixing screws and re-fix flush with the clad-

ding, using battens on to which you can fix metal-box mounting-flanges. Alternatively, you can purchase special mounting-boxes for use on boarded walls.

Timber wall cladding offers many possibilities for different designs, features and variations in appearance. For example, two recesses either side of a chimney breast can have a diagonal or chevron design in opposite directions. To ensure that the edges are all cut at exactly the same angle, use a sliding bevel tool which can be adjusted and locked off at the angle that you require. Always mark and cut on the face of each board. Keep the sawn ends clean by sanding the back edge of the cut only. Use a fine tenon saw (one with brass stiffening along its top edge) for best results.

Remove architraves around doors and windows, nail planed battens in position, fix the cladding to coincide with the edge of the batten and re-fix architraves. You might need a strip to cover the planed edge of the cladding depending on the finish. External corners can be butt-jointed where two pieces of timber are held together, not with a traditional joint, but with glue, nails or screws, and should have a cover strip or thin batten to hide and protect the gap between the two meeting pieces of wood. The professional finish is to chamfer each edge at 45° and glue the two edges to show no joint (when you're cladding vertically). Sometimes an attractive finish can be achieved by leaving a gap at the ceiling or skirting board. Use a narrow, straight batten as a temporary spacer to ensure a straight and even gap.

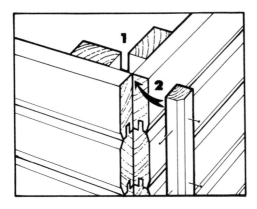

Vertical battens (**1**) are fixed for horizontal cladding. Form an attractive and protective corner by gluing and pinning a moulded prepared batten (**2**) to the end grain of the panelling. Horizontal panelling is fixed with the tongue uppermost and the groove slides on to it after nailing and punching through the inner corner of the tongue, so that no nails show.

## FIXINGS

The techniques of fixing are fairly easy to understand. The best possible way of fixing the battens is to drill, plug and screw them firmly. In a solid wall, you have to be certain that the screw has at least 1in (25mm) of hold in the wall, not just the plaster coating! Fixing to a stud partition wall is, of course, easier. But the same principle applies, that is, the screw must have at least 1in (25mm) purchase into the timber. The head of the screw needs to be countersunk beneath the surface of the batten. The best method of fixing the panelling boards to the battens is to 'secret-nail' them. Nail through the tongue of the panel using a thin moulding pin at an angle. Use a nail punch to get the head just below the surface of the wood, then the pin is covered by the groove of the next board. Each subsequent board is nailed in the same way. The same principles are involved when cladding a ceiling. Fix battens by screwing, never hammering, and never try to fix panelling on to plasterboard, or a lath and plaster ceiling, without battening-out first.

## FINISHES

Have you considered what finish you want to achieve? Manufacturers have been made aware of the increased interest in natural wood finishes in the DIY market recently, and a number of excellent products have appeared on the shelves of the DIY super-centres as a result. There are attractive coloured stains which the wood imbibes, allowing the natural beauty of the grain to be appreciated. Seals, varnishes and clear wood finishes are all available with full instructions.

## SUCCESSFULLY DIVIDING A ROOM WITH TWO WINDOWS

The average size living-room in a family house is often inadequate. Since the war there has been a trend to remove a dividing wall and convert two rooms into one, improving the appearance and available space. Conversely, as a family expands and grows or if a workroom or study is needed, a large front bedroom with two windows can be easily converted into two rooms. It may seem like a formidable task, but you really don't need to be a carpenter to build a stud partition wall. Once in place, insulated, boarded and decorated, it will look like a professionally built solid wall. By using a proprietary insulating material, you can also achieve good thermal and sound insulation properties.

## REGULATIONS

Before you start planning and buying materials, make a phone call to your local authority Building Control Officer. Tell him what you propose and ask him to come to your house by appointment to advise you. Regulations exist to ensure that safety and design standards conform to the minimum laid down regarding fire spread, durability and suitability. The officer will advise you on the regulations with reference to ventilation and natural light in each room. If you plan to use a divided room for kitchen, bathroom or WC then you must consult with the Environmental Health Officer.

There are a number of stipulations that you need to consider before deciding to construct the stud partition wall. The Building Control Officer will check the size of the openable window in each projected room, which must be related to the floor area of the new room. Consider, too, access to the second room. If privacy is required in the first room, a corridor will have to be constructed by building an extra stud partition wall, to make the rooms self-contained.

The next consideration is the position of the new stud partition wall in relation to the floor and ceiling joists. Obviously extra weight on a bedroom floor will require adequate support underneath that wall. Ideally the new partition wall will run at right angles to the floor and ceiling joists so that all the joists will share the extra load. You will not be bound to locate the wall at a specific point; however, you cannot build a new wall directly onto floorboards at a point between the joists when the new wall is to run parallel with the joists. Instead, locate directly over a particular joist. When the Building Control Officer visits you, ask him whether you will need to reinforce that particular joist (by bolting extra timbers either side of it). While you have the floorboards lifted, check and mark electric cables and pipe runs. Using a metal detector or a cable and pipe finder check the walls either side of the new wall, for possible pipes or cables buried in the plaster.

## CONSTRUCTING A STUD PARTITION WALL

A stud partition wall is constructed of pre-treated 4in × 2in (100mm × 50mm) sawn softwood. A timber frame is made up of tight fitting uprights called studs with shorter pieces nailed firmly between them to stabilize the whole frame. The shorter pieces are called noggings. The door frame will not be built in until the stud partition wall has been erected and made firm.

Measure and calculate the number of timbers to buy and have them delivered a week before you intend to build, so that they can stay in the room to acclimatize to the drier and warmer conditions. Check the illustration and use it as a guide to make a sketch of your own layout to scale. There are simple basic construction principles you must be aware of which will help overcome problems during construction: the head, or top timber, is screwed through the ceiling plaster into the joists above because nailing is too harsh a treatment for a ceiling; the end wall studs must be drilled, plugged and screwed firmly to the supporting walls; all studs must be cut very slightly over length, so they can be tightly wedged in place before securing.

Lay the bottom timber, or sole plate, on the floor in position, parallel to the facing wall, at right angles to its adjacent wall.

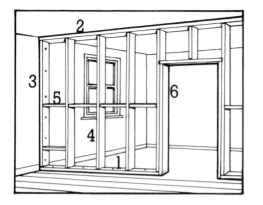

The component parts of a stud-partition wall are sole plate fixed to the floor (**1**), header fixed to the ceiling joists (**2**), vertical wall studs (**3**), studs (**4**), horizontal noggings (**5**) (where horizontal joints occur in the plasterboard), and door framing (**6**).

Draw guidelines either side of the flat 4in (100mm) timber. Use a spirit level or a plumb bob to continue the 4in (100mm) wide lines up each wall to the ceiling. The lines across the ceiling should now be vertically above the floor timber. Check with a timber held between them and a spirit level. A stud sensor will make the job very easy, otherwise use a nail to tap through the plasterboard until you find the centre of each joist. The nail holes can be filled and will be covered by the construction. Again check with the illustration to familiarize yourself with the fixing of the timbers either side of the door opening.

Screw the floor timbers into position first, either side of the measured door opening. Starting from the door opening, mark the positions of the studs so that their centres are 16in (400mm) apart. These measurements are to support 4ft- (1220mm-) wide plasterboards nailed upright. Lay the ceiling timber on the floor beside the floor timber and transfer the marks of the studs on to it. Now prop it into position and screw (through pre-drilled holes) into the joists. Cut the two side studs to a tight fit and drill, plug and screw them to the walls. Next, the studs either side of the door have to be fixed but not before a horizontal timber is housed in joints just above the door position. After the studs either side of the door have been cut and wedged into position, measure and mark on one stud a combined height of the door, the thickness of the door lining, a ¼in (6mm) gap at the top of the door, an allowance for floor coverings and another ¼in (6mm) gap. Use a spirit level to transfer this mark to the other stud. Remove both studs and lay them on the floor face up. Mark and cut a simple housing recess to take the 2in (50mm) head timber. Wedge each stud back into position and fix by skew nailing, having checked with a spirit level that they are vertical. Slot the horizontal door-head into the housing joints and nail from either side of the studs. Cut and fix two short stud pieces between the door-head and the ceiling timber. Cut and tightly fit the rest of the upright studs. If plasterboards are to be joined at their ends, cut and fix noggings to secure the ends. Between the top and bottom of a plasterboard one row of noggings is sufficient, but for added stability fix two rows. Note that at the door opening a second stud is fixed to the original studs between the floor and the door head. Once the door lining is fixed the door should have a gap of approximately ⅛in (3mm) each side.

## FIXING PLASTERBOARD

Plasterboard has a decorative side, which is ivory coloured and does not need to be skimmed with plaster, and a plastering side which is grey. To cut plasterboard, either use a fine-toothed hand saw or do it the professional way with a trimming knife. To make a straight cut across plasterboard use a straight-edge and a trimming knife. Cut on the face side, but not right through. With the edge of the board on the floor, fold the board back at the cut and run the trimming knife carefully down the back of the cut. Plasterboard nail indentations and gaps are easily covered with a plaster filler. While it is still firm, feather the edges to give a professional finish.

The first plasterboard is fixed flush to the inner stud of the door opening. Use galvanized plasterboard nails 6in (150mm) apart, and not too near the edge or the board will crumble. Above the doorway cut the plasterboard vertically to the centre of the main stud. The smaller piece of plasterboard above the door opening will share that stud for its fixing. Fit and fix all the boards on the one side first.

## INSULATING THE WALL

To insulate the wall cut to a tight fit 2in (50mm) polystyrene sheets, 2in (50mm) slabs of fibre glass or 2in (50mm) slabs of mineral wool. The insulation will be ineffective if a gap is left anywhere between the insulating material and the studs or noggings. Instructions for cutting and fitting come with the material. Remember that to solve a sound problem, the denser the material, the more effective the solution. Start covering the second side of the stud partition wall, again from the door opening. The edge of the plasterboards must line up flush with the inner stud face.

## FINISHING THE WALL

The ivory-coloured decorative side of a plasterboard is very simple to finish and does not need a plaster skim. If the boards are bevel-edged, buy a taping kit from your local DIY supercentre to seal and cover the joints. Minimal skill is required to apply the filler and to fix the covering tape with the plastic applicator. The edges are feathered off with a special sponge resulting in a perfectly flat surface. Once dry, the whole of the wall can be painted or wallpapered.

Door linings can be bought as a kit. The linings nailed to the studs will finish flush with the outer surfaces of both plasterboards covering the vulnerable edges. Fix the two side pieces first and then the header is wedged in between them and fixed with lost-head nails. Moulded architraves give a professional finish to the door opening and cover the gap between the door lining and the plasterboard. Use a mitre-box to cut the top corners and fix the architrave approximately ⅜in (10mm) from the face of the door lining. Fit and hang the door in its closed position, before fixing the door-stops tight to the door.

Matching skirting boards are available, as are picture rails and coving or cornices. Only the skirting board is an essential addition but even this can be built up using a square-edged floorboard and various mouldings, glued and pinned to the top edge. Other considerations to help in the construction are as follows. Instead of skew-nailing through the studs and noggings, you might consider cutting housing joints in the sole plate and the ceiling or head timber. An alternative is to butt-joint the studs and to use a metal framing anchor. This is a right-angled piece of metal, pre-drilled for screws, that has a diagonal fin to hold it rigid. If you have used flat-edged plasterboards, simply fill the joint with a proprietary plaster filler, but feather the edges when the filler is still firm to the touch. Make sure, too, that the joint between the new wall and the side wall is well filled.

## FITTING SERVICES IN A STUD PARTITION WALL

The illustration clearly shows you how to fit services in a stud partition wall. If cables or water pipes have to run horizontally, fix them at about 10in (250mm) above floor level and make a note of this for future reference. It is a safety principle that all electric cables

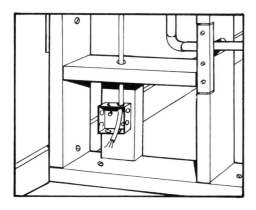 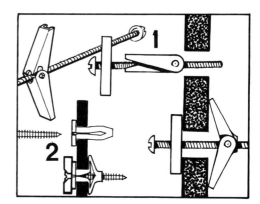

For running electric cables, ensure maximum safety by drilling ½in (12mm) holes in the centre of studs and noggings.

Fit extra timbers to hold electric mounting boxes. Run all pipework through holes drilled in the centres of studs and noggings or in notches protected by a recessed plate fixed flush with the front of the stud.

Two of the many cavity wall fixings that open out behind the drilled hole and grip the back of the plasterboard. The steel spring toggle (**1**) is closed to push it through the hole and as it clears the hole the arms fly apart to be drawn tight to the back of the board when the bolt is tightened on the fixing, which should only be lightweight. The hard plastic type (**2**) spreads out as the bolt is tightened.

should run vertically to and from switches and sockets. ½in (12mm) holes drilled in the centres of studs and noggings will ensure that the electric cables are safe from fixings. For holding electric mounting-boxes for sockets and switches, simply nail a tight-fitting nogging between the studs so that the mounting-box is fixed to the flat surface of the nogging. The front edge of the box must finish flush with the front face of the studs. Pipes are held in notches cut into the studs and a metal facing piece recessed into the face of the stud to hold and protect the pipe. The illustration shows more clearly how this is done.

To hang fixtures on a stud partition wall, it is always best to aim for the studs to achieve a firm fixing. If however you've planned to hang a cupboard in a certain position beforehand, then it is an easy job to fix extra studs and noggings to support the cupboard. Lightweight fixtures can be fixed to plasterboard using proprietary cavity wall fixings such as the spring-loaded toggle fixing, illustrated, or the plastic expanding plug. Cavity wall fixings are obtainable from all DIY stores and a leaflet is available to inform you what fixing is suitable for particular loads.

The same principle of construction is involved if a second stud partition wall has to be built to form a passage or corridor. This makes the first room smaller by approximately 3ft (a metre), but check with the local Building Control Officer as to width, ventilation and light source. Obviously the second partition will be built at the same time as the framework of the dividing stud partition wall, but ensure that there are extra studs at the intersection for adequate fixings. A second pair of hands is recommended to lessen the load and cut considerably the time spent on the job. A second 'friend' is your spirit level – make use of it often!

## CUTTING AND FITTING CERAMIC WALL TILES

Tiling changed from being strictly a trades-man's job to a DIY enthusiast's project with the introduction of new technology in tile manufacture, tiling tools and adhesives. It is now possible for anyone to create a beautiful, tough and hygienic wall finish. A new range of tiling tools helps to make any tiling job easy, speedy and enjoyable. Tile adhesive and grout are now combined in one tub for easy application. They give a smooth finish to the joints between tiles and contain anti-mould ingredient.

## PLANNING AND PREPARATION

Walls must be clean, dry, structurally sound and flat. Remove wallpaper with a steam stripper and allow the plaster to dry. Plaster walls that have not been sealed need a stabilizing solution. All bumps can be rubbed down and hollows filled with a one-coat plaster. To obtain a key on gloss painted surfaces, use a medium sandpaper over the whole surface. Scrape off any flaking paint and use a strong solvent washing-up liquid to degrease any suspect areas.

Plan your tiles to sit centrally if you are

tiling an entire wall. This leaves an equal space either side for the cut tiles. However, if you are tiling all around a window a full tile or a joint should be central on the window sill. Again this means that you have equal size cut tiles at each side of the window.

A simple aid to calculating how many tiles are needed and to help plot the exact position of the tiles on the wall is a DIY gauge-stick. Lay a piece of straight batten 1in × ½in (25mm × 12mm) on the floor and lay tiles along it in a straight line. Mark carefully on the batten the position of each tile and space or joint. If the tiles have spacing lugs, the spaces will be uniform and pre-set, otherwise use plastic spacers to give the cor-

rect positioning. Make a second gauge-stick if your tiles are not square. The gauge-stick can now be held against the wall, but use a spirit level to ensure vertical and horizontals are correct and the exact positions of tiles marked on the wall.

The easiest wall to tile is a plain one with no door or window. If you are tiling to the ceiling, plan to finish with full tiles at the top of the wall. The same applies to any tiled area – finish with full tiles at the top. Use the gauge-stick to mark the positions of the tiles from the ceiling to the skirting, where a cut tile will probably be needed. Nail a temporary long batten to support the lowest row of whole tiles. Use a spirit level before the final fixing. Find the centre of the wall and, with the aid of the gauge-stick, mark the positions of tiles and spacings as far as each

To help set out the walls correctly for tiling, use three battens: one marked out as a gauge-stick, the other two nailed to the wall at right angles to support the tiles. The gauge-stick must be marked very accurately by laying tiles and spacers on the floor against the stick. On a plain wall mark the centre of the wall for the first tiles. On a window wall, arrange the tiles centrally to the window.

Decide on either a tile or a joint to be the centre of the window sill. Under the sill arrange a row of full tiles. Matching plastic edging strip covers the cut edges of tiles and makes an attractive finish for external corners. Use a flexible mastic seal where tiles butt against a wooden window frame.

corner. Setting out tiles is very easy if you work carefully, and you'll find you now have equal cut tiles either side of the room. Using a spirit level nail another guide batten vertically where the first whole tile starts. The battens should now be at right angles to each other and should ensure a perfect finish.

When tiling around a window, as well as centring the tiles, plan a row of full tiles below the window sill. Another modern innovation is the use of matching edging strips to give an absolutely clean, neat edge to external corners. These exposed angles where horizontal and vertical tiles meet can now be made to look very professional with the use of this special tile trim. It can be obtained in all thicknesses and matching colours.

## LAYING THE TILES

To lift out the adhesive from the tub use a separate scraper tool. Spread it over an area of about a square yard (or square metre) and use the toothed spreader to form ridges by dragging it horizontally through the adhesive. The corner angle made by the guide battens is where the first tile must be laid.

Tile the area of the spread adhesive using the plastic spacers. These stay in position to be hidden when grouted over. Fix all full tiles first and wait the recommended time for the tile adhesive to set before removing the supporting battens.

## CUTTING TILES

Now you'll need to cut tiles to fit edges, borders and curved shapes as, for example, around a hand basin. Different cutters are designed for different tiles and the type of cut necessary. Straight cuts in standard ceramic wall tiles call for a simple low-cost carbide-tipped cutter. Use it with a straight-edge, but do take into account the thickness of the cutter. Matchsticks placed under either end of the scored line and pressure either side will give a clean, straight cut. For the slightly larger tiling job use a tool called a tile cutter and snapper. This is a medium-duty combined tool designed for easy and accurate cutting and snapping. Should you be left with about half a tile space vertically at the side of a door frame, the calliper in the tile-cutting set accurately measures the space and transfers it to each tile. This makes measuring and cutting quick and easy. This inexpensive device is foolproof, measuring and scoring with no fear of mistakes, and incorporates a snapping tool too.

For thick heavy-duty wall tiles, a lever-operated cutter makes the scoring and snapping child's play. This rugged, precision-engineered tool has been specially designed for the DIY market, but it is not expensive and is a must for those ambitious DIY tiling jobs.

Sometimes water pipes shoot out from a wall in the most inconvenient position! To cut around a pipe accurately and neatly need not be a problem. If the pipe is positioned at

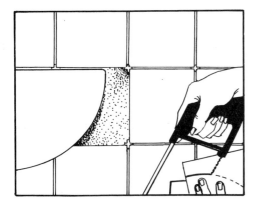

To cut a curve so that the tile fits accurately to a hand basin, cut a cardboard template to the exact shape of the space to be filled, then transfer the shape to the tile. A tile saw has a long-life, tungsten-coated carbide blade that cuts a full 360°, making it easy to cut curves. It can be used to cut tiles up to ⅜in (10mm) thick.

the edge of the tile, simply draw lines from the pipe's outer edges onto the tile, with a corresponding curve in the right position. Support the tile on the edge of the bench and cut around the curve with a tile saw. But it is more likely that the pipe position is somewhere in the centre of the tile! This problem is solved by cutting the tile in two at the pipe centre. Draw lines parallel with the outer edges of the pipe onto both halves of the cut tile and draw corresponding curves to match the shape of the pipe. Once again use a tile saw on both halves which, when stuck in position, will show little or no joint. To cut small slivers or tiny odd shapes use a tile-nipper tool. If an L-shaped tile is needed, it means cutting a square piece out of one of the corners. Mark up the two edges of the tile as the two sides of the cut and draw lines. Use a tile saw for the shortest cut and score the long cut with the scribe tool. Make use of the snapper tool to remove the corner piece from the tile, or use the lever-operated cutter for thicker tiles.

Curved cuts are just as easy but they do call for very accurate preparation work. To obtain a professional-looking finish on a cut tile against a curved basin, use a cardboard template. Cut a piece of card to the exact size of the tile that is to be cut and fixed against the basin. After cutting the curve with the scissors check that the template fits perfectly. Transfer the cardboard shape with a non-permanent felt pen to the tile to be cut. Support the tile on the edge of the bench and use a tile saw following the mark very carefully to ensure an accurate fit. All cut tiles can be tidied up with a special tile file.

## FINISHING OR GROUTING

Tile adhesives have particular drying times. Follow the manufacturer's instructions. The secret of a professional grouting job is to work quickly and only in small areas. Use a rubber grout spreader working in all directions. This is a very easy and satisfying part of the job. Wipe off excess grout with a damp sponge and use the joint finisher to obtain an even grout line. It is essential to use waterproof grout around baths and sinks. However, use a flexible silicone seal-ant around shower trays, between baths and wall tiles and at the top edge of a hand basin. Where tiles meet a wooden frame, for example at the back of a window sill, use a flexible sealant rather than grout. Once the whole area has been grouted and the excess removed, a fine film will be left on the surface of the tiles. This is actually helpful rather than a nuisance! When completely dry this fine powdery film is most effective as a polish to give a gleaming, brilliant finish to your professional tiling job.

## FILLING GAPS BETWEEN CEILINGS AND WALLS

Many older houses are now being bought, renovated and fitted with central heating. Older properties, previously heated by open fires, are now being subjected to new levels of humidity. Timber, especially flooring joists, suffers movement under these new conditions causing cracks to appear in ceilings.

Owners of newly built flats and houses also face problems. Kiln-dried new timber cannot possibly retain the ideal 12 to 15 per cent level of moisture content in a centrally-heated home. Estate agents and developers traditionally treat complaints about cracks appearing in plasterwork very lightly.

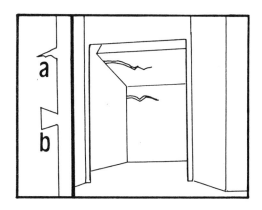

Sectional illustration shows (**A**) crack before it is raked out to form inverted V (**B**).

Unfortunately, it is one of the hazards of current speculative building. If you complain, you'll be told 'of course you'll get cracks, it's natural, it's just settlement!' To identify what has gone wrong, one needs to know a little about floor construction. (Read through the chapter on Floors, p.48.)

It is unlikely that a construction of mainly steel and concrete will suffer cracks in the plaster skim. If any do appear they are likely to be superficial. These hairline cracks should be raked out with a sharp knife and cut in an inverted 'V' shape. This makes the crack widest at its deepest point. By pushing filler hard into the crack it will form a key as in a dovetail joint. This will stop the filler, which should be mixed with emulsion paint, from falling out when it dries. By using a flexible filling knife correctly you should be able to obtain a very smooth finish. When it's almost dry, slightly dampen the surface to get a polished surface with the steel blade of the filling knife.

New, conventionally built houses, however, suffer cracks between ceilings and walls caused by stresses and movement in the timber part of the structure due to changes in temperature and humidity. Obviously, changes are constantly taking place so the problem needs to be solved with something more than the normal plaster filler.

Over the years, older houses become stabilized and settled within the limits of existing temperatures and humidity. With the introduction of central heating, timber loses a great deal of its moisture content. Shrinkage occurs in floor and ceiling tim-bers, as well as in stud partition walls. When there is movement in a structure, problems occur in the joint between the ceiling and wall. The crack is also more noticeable there because the eye is drawn to where light and shade is different and two surfaces meet.

## COVING

To solve this recurring problem in both new and older properties, manufacturers have produced the ideal DIY solution. Fixing attractive coving is not only a practical solution, it is also aesthetically pleasing, enhancing the look of a room. The package comes with a comprehensively illustrated leaflet, fully describing how to fix it.

What might appear to be a complicated part of the job, that is, accurately cutting internal and external mitred corners, is actually very simple thanks to a template included in the package to make cutting the coving foolproof.

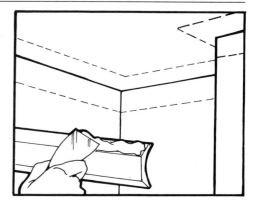

Measure right round the room and include the chimney breast and recesses. Make a rough sketch with these measurements and take it with you to your DIY supercentre. Choose the style and size of the cove to suit your particular room. Standard 4in (100mm) plaster cove is sold in lengths of 10 feet (3m), while 5in (125mm) cove comes in lengths of 10 feet (3m), 12 feet (3·6m) and 14 feet (4·2m). Work out all the lengths needed from your sketch first because it is quicker and easier to cut every length with its appropriate mitred angle before fixing any.

Pencilled guidelines drawn at the correct distance on the wall and ceiling will help to make the job of levelling the cove fairly

Draw guidelines along walls and ceilings 2⅝in (67mm) for 4in (100mm) girth cove and 3¼in (83mm) for 5in (127mm) girth cove from the angle of intersection. Scratch the areas to be in contact with the cove, providing a key for the adhesive. Use a mitre block or the special template provided to cut to length and to mitre the cove. Apply the adhesive about ⅛in (3mm) thick to the two surfaces the whole length of the cove.

simple. Provide a key for the adhesive by gently scratching inside the pencil marks, then brushing away all loose particles and dust. After cutting the mitres with the aid of either the template provided or a conventional mitre block, lightly sandpaper any

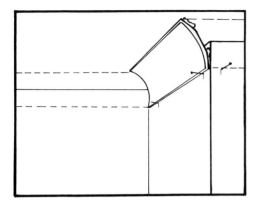

Gently position the cut cove between the guide-lines (two people should do this if the cove exceeds 6½ft (2 metres) in length). Remove the excess adhesive with a scraper and use it to make good joints and mitres. Draw a moistened brush along the joints. Small nails driven in below the cove support it whilst the adhesive is setting. The excess adhesive will fill in the holes later.

rough edges. Saw cuts must be made into the curve using a fine tooth saw.

For fixing lengths of more than 6½ feet (2m), it is advisable to use a helper. Alternatively, tack 1in (25mm) nails, about 18in (455mm) apart, along the line on the wall to use as support whilst pressing the cove into the adhesive. The nail holes will be filled later with the adhesive. Should any extra fixing be necessary, for example where the wall might be uneven, use galvanized plasterboard nails or alloy screws. Tap the nail heads just below the surface, but don't puncture the paper, and then fill with the cove adhesive. The adhesive must be mixed with water to the consistency recommended on the packet.

If the plaster to which the cove is to be fixed is very dry, dampen it with water just before offering up the cove. Mix sufficient adhesive for about half an hour's work, because it stays workable for about that time. Once in position, it will set hard in about an hour. The adhesive must be applied to the two surfaces that will be in contact with the wall and ceiling approximately ⅛in (3mm) thick. Excess adhesive can be wiped off, but at the same time fill in any gaps, mitres and joints. Before the adhesive begins to set, draw a wet paintbrush along the joints to give a clean, smooth finish.

Occasionally, it's necessary to terminate the end of the cove at a stairwell, or where a doorway extends to full ceiling height. This problem is solved by cutting a stop end. A mitre is cut at the end of an offcut, which is then cut off square. This piece will fit the

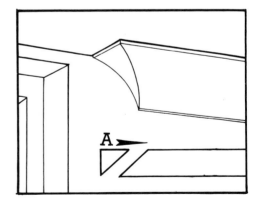

Where a window or door extends to ceiling height, cut stop-end or wedge-shaped end piece to terminate the cove. Cut the external mitre, then cut it off square to fit the prepared end, as illustrated (**A**).

end of the cut length of cove to give a very professional finish.

Should the cove need to run around the interior of a bay window wall, first cut squared-off lengths to fit each wall. Pencil marks drawn around each piece on the ceiling will intersect. A line drawn between the intersecting marks will give the cutting line on each piece of cove. The illustration will make this part of the operation very simple to follow.

Gyproc cove has an ivory-coloured surface similar to the decorative side of a plasterboard. But the cove is not suitable for skimming with plaster. It has an excellent surface finish which should be primed with a PVA-based primer to seal the surface, ready for your chosen finish.

Covering cracks is not the only practical reason for using coving: it can also hide electrical circuits and pipes. Interior designers and decorators use curved plaster coving as a decorative feature. By the clever use of battens and tube lighting, attractive diffused lighting effects are possible.

A curtain rail fixed close to the ceiling joint presents no problems at all when fixing cove. Use a very simple arrangement with two long battens and the cove fixes to the vertical one to make a very attractive pelmet.

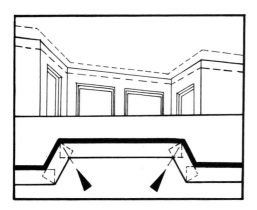

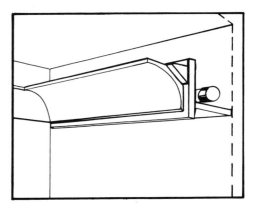

The illustration shows a bay with the lengths of cove in position before the mitres are cut and showing the angle of cuts – arrowed. Draw pencil marks on the ceiling (67mm for 4in or 83mm for 5in) from the walls and parallel to them. Position a piece of cove with square ends and mark it on the wall edge where the walls meet and on the ceiling edge where the lines on the ceiling intersect. Cut the cove along a line drawn between the two marks.

Fix a length of prepared timber between the side walls. Screw to it a vertical piece to give a minimum 2in (50mm) to the ceiling. Fix a triangular fillet in position to which the cove is fixed. Tube lighting is hidden in the box.

This can be mitred at either end to join the side walls as a continuous run.

Some rooms lend themselves to a more

decorative form of moulding. A range of coving accessories is available for use with the standard plaster cove. Some of the accessories are extremely useful as well as attractive. Corner pieces for internal and external use completely eliminate the need for any mitring. The internal corner piece, for example, is fixed into the corner with standard cove adhesive and then the square-cut coving is pushed tightly to it. External corner pieces around chimney breasts fit just as easily. Made from a nontoxic, noncombustible plaster, they're strong, durable and add interest to the coving feature. The addition of a central, moulded ceiling-rose could totally transform the look of a room.

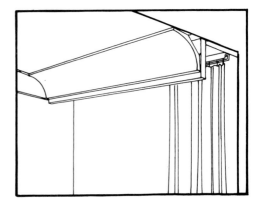

Pelmet is made up of two timbers and fixed to ceiling joists. Curtain rail hidden in box which together with ceiling fixing supports cove.

# CHAPTER SIX

# DOORS

# AND

# WINDOWS

## DOOR PROBLEMS

Fitting a new carpet is usually a job for a professional tradesman. There are, though, advanced DIYers with sufficient skill, expertise and the specialist tools needed, who are able to cut and fit a new carpet in a room, if its shape is uncomplicated. However, all DIYers can successfully tackle the related jobs of removing the old floor covering, de-nailing the wooden floor, cleaning off old lumps of plaster and paint and, of course, dusting and vacuuming. Skirting boards suffer a great deal of bumping and scraping during the course of the day, so a very worthwhile job to carry out before fitting a new carpet, is to rub down and paint them. The door will probably also need attention.

It is unlikely that the door to the room will already have the required minimum floor clearance of a ½in (12mm). Thicker carpets with a heavier underlay will obviously require more space under the door before the carpet is laid, so the door will have to be rehung so that it will glide over the carpet without dragging on it. In most cases all that is needed to lift the door over the new carpet is to swap the existing hinges for two-piece 'rising-butts'. These hinges lift the door as it

opens. Each hinge comes in two parts: one part is flap or leaf with a solid vertical pin. This is screwed to the door frame, never the other way round! The second half of the hinge has a hollow knuckle, which is fixed to the door. The door is lifted and dropped into position with the pin sliding into the hollow knuckle. If you are able to buy brass rising-butt hinges of exactly the same size as the existing hinges the job will be made much easier. As rising-butt hinges must be fixed with the pin half to the door frame you must buy hinges to suit your door, opening either left- or right-handed. A simple method of checking is to look at the countersunk screw holes in the half that has the pin. A left-hand door opening will have the pin on the right-hand side and a right-hand opening the other way round.

Don't attempt to re-use the existing screw holes; you'll end up with at least one screw head angled, causing the door to bind when closed. Glue into the screw holes tight fitting wooden plugs so that new pilot holes can be made exactly where they are required. Adjustments to a hinge recess can be made with a paring chisel if it's too small, or by fitting a cardboard 'shim' if it's too deep.

The next stage is to plane off a small triangular shape from the top outside corner of the door as illustrated. It sounds drastic but it is absolutely necessary! If that small bevel was not removed, the top corner of the door would jam underneath the frame, not allowing sufficient 'lift' to lower the door hinge onto the pin of the post hinge. Plane inwards from the outer edge of the door. Planing from the centre towards the edge would split the timber because you are planing end grain. When the door is closed the bevel will be tucked in behind the doorstop and be completely hidden.

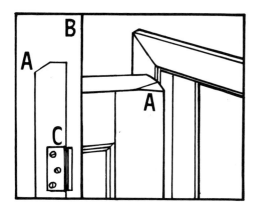

Fit rising-butt hinges so that the door lifts up as it opens over a carpet. Without a slight bevel at (**A**) planed as shown in the illustration, the door would not clear the frame as it opens. The section (**B**) shows the bevel (**A**) in relation to the hinge position (**C**). Plane in from the edge to avoid splitting the end grain of the wood.

Prop the door into position using two tiny wedges under the door to check that the door hinge recesses line up with the door post hinge recesses. With luck the hinges will line up perfectly. On the other hand you might find that the door hinge recesses are about ⅛in (3mm) higher than the others and the top of the door touching the frame. If this is the case it is necessary to remove exactly ⅛in (3mm) from the bottom of the door. This will bring the recesses back into line.

Score a line with a trimming knife parallel with the floor to give the correct clearance from the floor. When removing the strip of timber, plane inwards from either edge into the centre. Paint or seal the bottom edge of the door to prevent moisture penetration. If only ⅛in (3mm) has to be removed from the bottom of the door this is easy with a plane. If, however, more than say ¼in (6mm) has to be removed, use a sharp hand saw and finish it off with a smoothing plane. Before fitting the hinges, wedge the trimmed door into position to make absolutely certain that you have the right clearance of ⅛in (3mm) all around the door. Keep marking and planing where necessary.

Once both halves of the rising-butts are fitted and the door lowered into position, the latch or lock should click to close. Any minor adjustment that might be necessary can be done by removing the striking plate from the door post and repositioning it. Use charcoal, wax crayon or a piece of carbon paper on the end of the latch or bolt. This will enable you to mark the door post or jamb when the door is closed, to show where the new position of the striking plate should be. Make the mortice slightly larger and if necessary the striking plate recess too. With the striking plate repositioned the door should now click into position to fit tightly against the door stops.

## STICKING DOORS

Great care must be taken when painting doors! Whereas the technique of 'laying off' paint ensures that a thin film is left on the surface of the door, often a build-up occurs at the hidden back edge. If the back edge is overlooked or neglected then a build-up of as much as ⅛in (3mm) can occur. When hard and dry the paint has effectively increased the width of the door and will cause it to bind or even prevent it from closing. This problem can be solved by using a paint scraper very gently to remove the build-up. Use two grades of glass paper to smooth down the area before applying a thin coat of primer and finishing coats.

When you think of it, a door suffers a great deal of punishment throughout its life! It can be swung about dozens of times a day and as a consequence door furniture, fittings and screws undergo a great deal of banging; metal parts wear, and screws distort, rust or loosen. So if a door sticks when closing, check that the screws holding the face plate or those holding the keeper plate in the door jamb are not loose. If they are the problem is easily solved!

Ideally the gap between a door and its frame should be constant, but if there is sticking or rubbing then there are obviously tight spots. If these are on the locking edge of the door top or bottom, you might be able to plane these off without removing the door, except of course for the part nearest the floor. However, it could be that the screws holding the hinges have become loose causing the door to bind on its leading edge. Remove the screws two at a time and replace with longer screws of the same gauge or glue wooden plugs into the holes and drill new pilot holes for new screws.

If you've noticed that the door binds against the locking door post as it closes, you'll probably find too large a gap at the hanging edge. To solve this problem you'll need to cut the hinge recesses slightly deeper. It is better to pare off slight shavings rather than take too much off at one go! Keep checking and fitting until you have successfully created a uniform gap around the door

If on the other hand the gap at the hinge edge is very tight, causing the door to bind there as it closes, the depth of the hinge recesses needs to be reduced. This is the easiest of DIY jobs because it simply means cutting a piece of cardboard shim to fit the recess. This has the effect of pushing the door away from the hinge joint and opening up the gap.

## SLIDING SASH WINDOWS

Many more older properties are being restored these days. People are appreciating that it is more important to restore than replace. Provided that there is no rot present, it is always worth preserving well-designed features of yesteryear. For example, sliding sash windows are a common feature of houses built in the last century and the modern UPVC windows and frames with which they are often replaced can look out of place in a traditional Victorian or Georgian front elevation. Sash windows, less common these days, still need maintenance. Jobs such as the renewal of parting beads, tightening up of staff beads and sash cord replacement are all made easier by first understanding how a sash window works.

## HOW A SASH WINDOW WORKS

Take time to check the details of the illustrations and you'll find that the box frame, which houses the sliding sashes, is not the mystery you might have thought it to be. The pocket cover is easily removed to expose the long iron weights supported by the sash cords. The staff beads prise off quite easily and, because they're mitred at the corners, you'll need to spring them out from the centre first. Unless you need to take off all the staff beads to re-fix them more tightly to stop rattles, just release one side staff bead. This will allow you to ease out the lower sash.

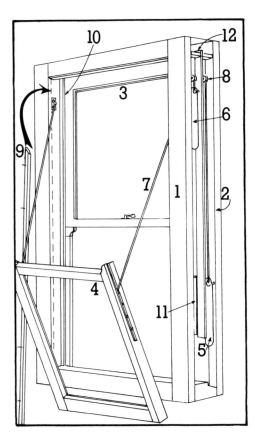

The principle of a sliding sash window is not difficult to understand. The heavy weights housed in a hollow on each side of the window balance the weight of each of the sashes. Weights and windows are joined

Component parts of a vertical sliding sash window: (**1**) Inner lining (**2**) Outer lining (**3**) Top sash (**4**) Lower sash (**5**) Top sash weight (**6**)) Lower sash weight (**7**) Cord (**8**) Pulley (**9**) Staff bead (**10**) Parting bead (**11**) Pocket (**12**) Parting slip (separating weights).

Prise off staff bead (**9**) by inserting a wide chisel behind it in a central position so that it is sprung out of ends. The lower sash is then easily slid forward to start the cord replacement job. Always replace both cords.

to each other by the sash cords. As you lift or lower one of the sashes the weight moves up and down inside its box. This method of counterbalance allows the window to stay in any position without dropping. Check the diagram to familiarize yourself with all the different parts of a sliding sash window. Because there are more parts to a sliding sash than a traditional casement window there is obviously more to go wrong. Pulleys can wear out or seize up, metal catches lose tension if the sash is loose and rattles, but the most common problem is a worn or broken sash cord. Fortunately this is the easiest problem to solve.

## REPLACING A SASH CORD

Sash cords will obviously wear over the years and should be replaced as soon as signs of wear are evident before a break occurs. Never replace just one that's worn or broken, it's always worth doing both at the same time.

In carrying out this repair you'll soon learn everything there is to know about sash windows because you'll have to handle practically every component! But it is relatively easy, especially if you have a second pair of hands available. Buy a hank of good quality sash cord, so that you have it to hand for an emergency. Sash cord is available in many different types but pre-stretched polyester will give excellent service for many years.

Having removed curtains and prised off one of the upright staff beads with a chisel (taking care not to damage the frame), tap the points of the nails back into the wood. This is to ensure safety and to be ready for re-fixing. If layers of paint are holding the bead in position, use a trimming knife to score a straight line to cut through the paint. The upright staff bead is long and flexible and springs out quite readily, because the ends are mitred, that is, cut at 45°. Now it's easy to swing the inner lower sash towards you into the room. It can move and swing unexpectedly because the weights are still attached so take care with the glazing. The long, narrower bead between the two sliding sashes, now exposed, is the parting bead. It is held by a tight push-fit into a slot or channel at either side of the frame. It may

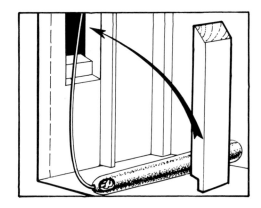

The pocket piece can be removed after lifting out the parting bead from its groove. This gives access to the weight. Some pocket pieces are screwed into place so take care not to split the wood if paint or filler has been used to hide the screw head. Then, lifting out each pocket piece, mark it R or L. Sometimes weights differ for outer and inner sashes so mark them as they are removed.

possibly be pinned in place with small panel pins but should come out fairly easily without breaking. The outer sash can now also be swung into the room.

On each side of the inner frame about 6in (150mm) up from the sill is located the pocket cover which seals the weight compartment. It is about 10in long × 2in wide (250mm × 50mm). Carefully insert a chisel to prise it forward once the parting bead has been removed. If a screw or nail holds it in position take care not to split the covers when removing them. You'll see that they are strangely chamfered, which is to ensure that they go back the correct way. It's a good idea to mark right and left with a pencil on the back of each cover as you remove them.

In order to handle the sashes comfortably and to be able to cut the cords, secure each cord (where they emerge over the pulley near the top of the frame) by nailing them in a position where the staff bead will eventually cover the nail holes. Support the sash before cutting the cords underneath the fixing point. Now make a note of how the cord is fixed to the sash. It will either be threaded through a hole and tied in a knot, or nailed in a channel at the side of the sash itself. Don't throw the cord away because that piece and the rest of the sash cord will give you the exact length to cut the new sash cord. Tie a piece of thin string to the free end of the cord which is still attached to the weight. A double hitch is the best, so that it is not impeded as it runs over the pulley and will hold firmly. Pull out the nail holding the cord to the frame and ease the weight out through the pocket. Untie the cord from the weight and keep it. Now draw the string over the pulley by pulling on the old cord.

You have to use the string to pull the new sash cord back into the pocket and over the pulley. Tie a temporary knot in the cord at the pulley end to stop it shooting back over the pulley! Tie the other end on to the weight.

A cautionary note follows! Check the measurement from the channel in the side of the sash to the glass. If you have to use nails to secure the new cord they should be a ¼in (6mm) less than the measurement you have just taken! Otherwise the glass is going to shatter. If the original cord was knotted fix the new cord the same way.

There's no need to despair if the original sash cord is broken. A simple method of feeding the new sash cord over the pulley to the weight is to use a 'mouse': a small weight is tied to the string and fed over the pulley to drop to the bottom of the box. Builders use a miniature version of a bicycle chain or a small piece of lead tied to the string, but any small weight, even a nail, will work. Once the string is through the new sash cord can follow.

Sometimes owners of older properties are dismayed to find that cords are actually missing on windows that have been semi-permanently fixed with screws or nails! To measure a new cord accurately, follow these instructions. Lift out the sash and measure the length of the cord groove in the side of the window. Mark that measurement on the frame itself, measuring from the top down. Following the instructions given above, tie the long new cord to the weight and pull on the cord so that the weight hangs 2in (50mm) above the bottom of the pocket box or compartment. Hold the tensioned cord against your mark on the frame and cut it.

Pull on the cord so that the weight arrives at the top to be supported by pushing a wedge of wood over the pulley. This will stop the cord from slipping back. Do the same thing to replace the second cord. Fix the cords to the sashes, take out the wedges and slide the sashes back into position. Check the movement of the sashes and ensure that the weights do not bounce against the bottom of the compartment box. If adjustments are necessary, it's very easy to shorten the cord by re-tying at the weight end. If you find a piece of wood dividing the weights in the box compartment, check that the weights slide each side of it without impediment.

### Renewing beads

You will have checked the condition of the parting beads and the staff beads which, over the years, suffer as much as sash cords. These beads are inexpensive and when renewed give the whole window a new lease of life. Use oval nails for fixing; punch the heads just below the surface and use a wood filler.

### A rattling sliding sash window

The problem of a rattling sliding sash window can easily be overcome by prising off the staff beads and moving them closer in to the sliding sash before re-fixing. The central parting bead that separates the two sliding sashes can also be prised out and replaced when worn. The sash cords run over brass pulleys, which should be maintained in good condition and kept free-running.

Make a note of these points and remember them when going through the illustrations. All sash cords and weights must be in place

The pulley must be kept free from paint and dirt. Oil it occasionally to keep it running freely. The cord is fixed into a groove cut into the side of the sash but the top nail fixing must be lower than the centre of the pulley measuring from the top of the pulley stile in which it is fixed.

before fitting the top sash first. Pulleys should not be painted. Clean up and polish any that have been, and use penetrating oil to release a jammed pulley wheel. Notice that the cords are not nailed all the way up in the groove but only for the bottom 6in (152mm). Knock nails into the beads on the bench before offering them into position. When replacing a staff bead push it tightly against the sash and ease it away very slightly before driving the nails home.

Having successfully replaced one set of sash cords, you will no longer have any feelings of trepidation when tackling the next. Remember that time spent on the preparation of the job is most important and easy! The result will be both professional and long-lasting.

# CHAPTER SEVEN

# PLUMBING

## COMMON PLUMBING PROBLEMS AROUND THE HOME
## GURGLING WATER AND AIR FROM TAPS

Air in the water system is troublesome but there are precautions that can be taken to prevent it getting there in the first place. In poorly designed systems air locks may occur during normal use. However, the most likely cause is that air has entered the system after it has been drained and refilled. Sometimes it is advisable to drain the plumbing system completely if you intend to leave the house unoccupied during the winter months. On your return you'll need to re-fill it.

To avoid the possibility of air locks forming whilst the system is filling connect one end of a hose to a cold water tap on a mains supply and the other end to the drain-cock on the hot water system. Open both the draincock and the tap; magically the cistern will fill from the bottom and air will naturally be pushed in front of the rising water. This is for a a direct cylinder hot-water system having no central heating.

If you plan to leave your house for a spell during the winter it is imperative to protect the plumbing and central heating systems. Switch off the boiler and immer-sion heaters, drain the hot-water cylinder, turn off the mains at the stopcock, flush the WCs and run water from the taps. In order that you do not have the job of draining the central heating system, add an anti-freeze solution via the header tank but follow the manufacturer's directions exactly. Water standing in WC pans and waste traps should have salt added to it to prevent it freezing. It's always advisable, of course, to have a friend or relative check the house periodically, especially to add a little salt or water to the traps in case of drying out. If too much water is lost from any trap, foul smells will enter the house from the sewage system.

If the plumbing system has been poorly designed, a pipe of too small a diameter might be found feeding the hot water storage cylinder. Normally it is ¾in (20mm) and at this bore, replacement cold water will not be allowed to fall in the vent pipe, when hot water is drawn. If the level is allowed to reach the horizontal supply pipe in the hot water system air will be drawn into the pipe and an air lock formed.

If a full system is being refilled, when all taps and draincocks are closed and the main stopcock opened, check that there are no sluggish ball valves. This can be another reason for trapped air in the system.

All these reasons can be checked and put right but the symptoms are all the same – a poor flow of water, bubbling and spluttering from a hot water tap and the possibility of complete failure of the system, so that no water is available when the tap is turned on. Now all this sounds as if it's a job for a plumber and his bag of tricks, but it need not be! It is a simple DIY job for you with a length of garden hose! The trick is to use mains pressure from your cold tap over the kitchen sink to blow the air bubble out of the system. Firmly secure one end of the hose to the kitchen sink tap or any other tap on mains water pressure, and the other end to the affected problem tap. Open both taps and in a short while the higher pressure from the mains water will force out the air bubble. You might have to repeat this two or three times to get all the air out of the system. Remember that a long length of hose can contain a lot of water, so take care when removing it!

## LEAKING OVERFLOW PIPES

When water runs continuously from an overflow pipe, it can cause many problems: walls become damp, and mould and algae grow; soil is eroded; nasty accidents can occur when it is allowed to freeze on a path or patio. With the thought of upheaval and disruption in the back of one's mind, it's so easy to put off calling in a plumber. However, not only are most WC cisterns or storage tanks easily accessible, they are also not difficult to repair and service. Understanding the basic design features of a ball valve cistern and how it operates will help you gain confidence to tackle the replacement of a washer, a diaphragm in a modern cistern or a float valve. Ball valves supply and maintain a level of water in WC cisterns, cold water storage cisterns and expansion tanks. The ball or float is connected to the valve by the arm. It's a very simple piece of engineering which works efficiently most of the time. When the water level falls in the cistern or tank, you'll see the ball or float falling with it. At this point water gushes through the valve to fill the cistern or tank. When the water reaches a prescribed level, with the ball floating on its surface, this action forces the valve mechanism to close, stopping the supply of water. If the water continues to run and rise in the tank, it will reach what is effectively the safety outlet. Without the overflow pipe, water would continue to rise over the edge of the tank and cause very serious problems. Water dripping outside from an overflow pipe usually indicates a faulty ball valve.

See, from the diagrams, the difference between an older-type ball valve, such as a Portsmouth valve, and a modern diaphragm ball valve. If yours is the older type with the brass body, it's quite easy to replace the small washer housed in the flanged washer cap. Constant opening and closing of the slotted plug which houses the washer causes a great deal of wear and the washer will need to be replaced from time to time.

Start by closing the stopcock to shut off the water supply. There should be one located close to the storage tank. A screw-on cap is sometimes found at the end of the valve body and this must be removed. A split pin holds the float-arm to the body of the valve, which must also be removed, enabling the cranked end of the float arm to be pulled clear of the slot in the plug. The plug (piston) can now be pulled free of the body of the valve. By holding a screwdriver through the slot in the plug you can unscrew the cap which holds the washer. Use a pair

of pliers but protect the brass from the jaws of the pliers with a piece of cloth. Ease out the old washer from the cap, but clean the piston, especially where the pliers held it, with fine wire wool. If the plug does not have a removable cap housing the washer, use a sharp skewer to pick out the worn washer. It isn't difficult to wriggle the new washer underneath the flange in the plug. Smear the plug with vaseline and carefully clean the inside of the valve body. Do this by wrapping a piece of fine abrasive paper around a pencil and using this to remove

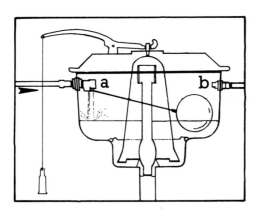

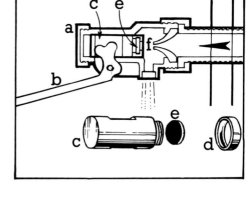

An older type ball valve, the Portsmouth, in a cast iron cistern. The flushing action starts when the bell is raised by pulling the chain and water is forced inside it as it falls. The water rises to cover the inside stand pipe and the siphonic action starts as the water rushes down the flush pipe to the pan. The ball-float falls and the arm opens the valve at (**A**) allowing water to refill the cistern. A fault with either the valve or the ball float would allow water to continue to run until it reaches the level of the 'overflow' pipe (**B**) which is the safety factor in all cisterns and storage tanks.

Overflowing pipes are often the result of faulty valves. Illustrated is a Portsmouth valve showing an enlarged detail of the piston (**C**) and washer (**E**) used for years until the 'diaphragm' was introduced. To renew a faulty washer turn off the stopcock controlling the supply of water to the cistern, then unscrew the end cap (**A**) and pull out the split pin so that the arm (**B**) can be detached. Slide out the piston (**C**) and unscrew the cap (**D**) in which the washer is housed. Renew it and reverse the procedure. The washer seals by pressing against the valve seat (**F**).

any corrosion or hard water scale. Re-assemble the parts in reverse order.

After restoring the water supply you'll probably have to adjust the ball-valve arm in order to maintain the water at the level indicated on the inside body of the cistern. Having replaced the washer in the ball valve, you might be lucky enough to find that another source of annoyance, the problem of 'water-hammer' has been eliminated!

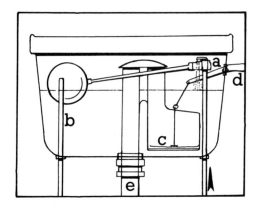

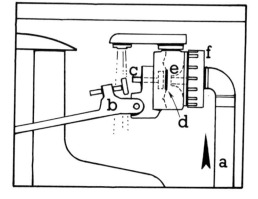

A modern direct action WC cistern is flushed by pressing on a lever or handle (**D**). A perforated metal or plastic plate is raised inside the siphon tube on which there is a thin plastic diaphragm or flap valve (**C**). Water is forced up over the bend and down the flush pipe (**E**) causing a siphonic action. Both supply pipe (**A**) and overflow pipe (**B**) are located in the base of the cistern. If the ball float is faulty or the arm not properly adjusted water will rise up over the overflow pipe (**B**) and cause problems outside the house.

The ball float activates the pivoted end of the arm (**B**) on which is fixed a plastic disc. This presses a 'plug' (**C**) which closes the water supply by pushing firmly a diaphragm (**D**) against the valve seat (**E**). The water supply pipe (**A**) is located in the base of the cistern. To replace a faulty diaphragm in a modern cistern stop the water supply first by turning off the controlling stopcock. Unscrew the large retaining nut (**F**) so that the old diaphragm can be picked out and renewed.

## NOISE AND VIBRATION PROBLEMS IN COLD WATER STORAGE TANKS

Banging or steady drumming noises in pipes or in cold water storage tanks are often the result of a worn washer in a ball valve (*see above*). The incessant drumming noise that is often heard after hot water has been drawn off happens when water flows in to refill the tank. As water rushes into the tank ripples are caused on its surface. These can cause the ball and valve to bounce. When the valve bounces on its seating, it produces water-hammer noises. Sometimes a banging noise is heard in pipes when a certain tap is turned on. In this case, the cause is probably a worn tap-washer not closing properly on its seating. It might also be that the metal 'shoulder' or seating is worn and needs a DIY reseating tool to level it. This is a very simple job carried out with an inexpensive reseating tool which comes with full instructions.

### Replacing the valve

If the water-hammer problem has not been solved by replacing the washer in the ball valve, then the problem of fluctuating water pressure can be overcome by replacing the valve.

The valve is held securely in the cistern body and connected to the copper supply pipe by inner and outer fixing nuts. The first nut on the supply pipe is called a tap connector and this needs to be unscrewed with a spanner to disconnect it from the valve stem.

Ball valves are marked LP, MP or HP. They are manufactured specifically to suit different water pressures, low, medium or high. If the cistern is fed from the mains, a HP valve is essential. However, most WC cisterns are fed from a cold-water storage tank, in which case the pressure is low and an LP valve should be fitted.

Having chosen a ball valve to suit the water pressure, close the stopcock to stop the supply of water to the cistern. After loosening the tap connector as previously indicated, remove the float arm and unscrew the outer fixing nut so that you can pull out the valve. It's always a good idea to replace the washers either side of the cistern body. Push the new valve into position and re-assemble the tap connector and tighten all fixing nuts. Double check that the tap connector and the valve are all aligned and all nuts tightened.

## UNBLOCKING WASTE PIPES, TRAPS AND WCS
## WASTE PIPES AND TRAPS

The tantalizing aroma of a joint of roast pork or lamb may activate the taste buds, but the resulting coagulated fat can spell disaster for the waste system below the kitchen sink! Greasy roasting trays and dinner plates should be allowed to cool, and the fat scraped off and disposed of in a plastic bag rather than swilled off down the kitchen sink before cleaning. Hot water only melts the grease and fat momentarily. Once it hits the cold water in the trap, it hardens and stays there. Other debris will build up until a serious blockage occurs. If less and less water is draining away on successive days,

then a complete blockage is not far away. Regular use of a mild, chemical drain cleaner will prevent the build-up of debris in the bottom of the trap.

If a complete blockage has occurred, try using a 'force cup' or sink plunger to force the debris through into the waste pipe. The plunger is a rubber or plastic cup mounted on to a wooden handle. Run 2 to 3in (50 to 75mm) of water into the sink, hold a damp cloth tightly against the overflow outlet to cover it and with the rubber cup held tightly over the waste, pump it with the handle until the water begins to clear. If bubbles blow back from the rim of the plunger smear it with vaseline to improve the seal. Continue to pump until the blockage is cleared and the water flows normally.

A more expensive but more efficient tool is the compressed air gun. It will not only fit the waste of the kitchen sink but also comes with adaptor nozzles to suit various waste sizes. The nozzle is placed into the waste outlet and by use of the hand pump a pressure is built up to clear the blockage. A trigger action releases the compressed air, which can be controlled. If more pressure is needed, extra strokes of the hand pump build up the pressure in the cylinder.

All sink and basin traps have an access cap for rodding and cleaning, and the trap itself can be unscrewed quite easily for cleaning purposes. Place a plastic bucket underneath the trap before unscrewing the plug. Should the blockage be located further along the waste pipe, an inexpensive drain auger can be passed into the waste pipe to clear the blockage. An auger is a long length of coiled wire which is very flexible and will pass through small holes. It is rotated with a cranked handle to clear blockages at a distance from the sink.

Modern plastic traps can be either of the screw type or have joints that push and fit

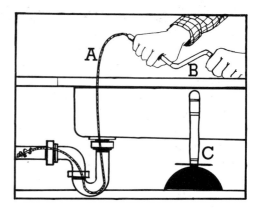

To clear blockages well down in a waste pipe try using a flexible drain auger (**A**). This length of coiled wire will pass through the smallest diameter hole and easily find its way into the waste pipe to clear any blockage. By cranking the handle (**B**) the corkscrew end will dislodge debris; pull and push the auger and run water to free the pipe. For a blocked trap as an alternative use a 'force cup' (**C**), but cover the overflow outlet with a damp cloth.

together. Each is easy to dismantle, so when you disconnect a trap the water that had been trapped in the sink will flow through the waste into the bucket. After cleaning out the trap reassemble, but do test for leaks.

## WCs

We are taught at a very early age what should and should not be flushed down the lavatory pan! If the water rises in the pan and subsides only slowly, it's most likely to be the result of somebody's carelessness or neglect. A larger plunger similar to the sink force cup will usually clear a blockage or

obstruction. If it doesn't, rent a WC auger. The auger operates on the same principle as the sink auger. The flexible coiled wire is rotated by a rod in a hollow tube and a cranked handle fixed to the rod at the top end.

Use rubber gloves and disinfectant to protect the floor area around the WC.

## PROBLEMS WITH TAPS

Staining on a bath or sink caused by a continuously dripping tap is easily removed by a proprietary brand of bath cleaner. Apply it with a brush, leave it for the recommended time then wash it and the stains away.

Most people think that the only cause of water dripping from a tap is a worn washer which needs replacing. However, check that water is not leaking from beneath the head of the tap when it is turned on. If it is, then it's not the washer that is worn but the pack-

ing inside the gland which needs to be picked out and replaced to seal the gland completely. Drips from the spout may also be caused by a worn shoulder or seat. The washer sits on the shoulder and is compressed when the tap is turned, to stop the flow of water.

The two most common types of taps are pillar taps (also called bib taps) and reverse-pressure taps.

## WASHER PROBLEMS ON PILLAR TAPS

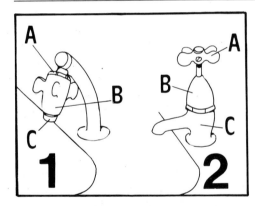
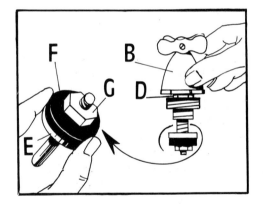

Tap 1 is a typical reverse-pressure type. To replace the washer the water supply need not be turned off and only one retaining nut (**A**) has to be unscrewed. The body (**B**) then drops down to expose the jumper and washer which drop out of the body when the nozzle (**C**) is tapped on the floor. Remove the jumper and washer for easy replacement and reassemble.

Tap 2 is a common pillar tap where the mains water must be turned off to open it up. (**A**) is the capstan head, (**B**) the shroud or sheath and (**C**) the body.

Remember to turn off the supply and put the plug into the waste before you start! To replace a worn washer in a pillar tap first turn off the stopcock, then unscrew the shroud (**B**) taking care to protect the chrome. Use a spanner to loosen the head-gear nut, just above the main body of the tap (**D**) which releases the whole of the assembly including the jumper (**E**) and washer (**F**). Unscrew the small holding nut (**G**) which allows the washer to be prised off and replaced. If it's rusted on, it's just as easy to replace the jumper and washer with new ones.

Replacement washers for all types of taps are fairly standard and it makes sense to keep a stock handy. Before dismantling and repairing a pillar tap, turn off the supply to that tap, put the plug into the waste and a thick towel in the sink or handbasin. Drain the pipe feeding the tap and then open up the valve as far as it will go as if turning on the water. A pillar tap will have a domed cover which has to be unscrewed first. A strap wrench is the ideal tool for this, otherwise use an ordinary wrench but protect the chrome. The head-gear nut, just above the main body of the tap, can then be un-screwed and the whole of the head-gear assembly lifted out. You'll find the washer fixed to a jumper, which in some cases comes away with the head-gear, but in some taps will be lying inside the tap body. The washer is either held securely by a nut or pressed over a rivet-like end of the jumper. Occasionally the nut can't be unscrewed without damaging the jumper, in which case replace the jumper and washer together. Otherwise, fit a new washer and replace the retaining nut. Lower the head-gear back into the base of the tap, tighten the head-gear nut and reassemble the chrome cover.

## WASHER PROBLEMS IN A REVERSE-PRESSURE TAP

This upside-down or 'supatap' is sometimes called the DIYer's gift because there is no need to stop the supply of water to the tap when the washer has to be replaced. These taps are actually turned on and off by turning the nozzle of the tap. Replacing a washer in the reverse-pressure tap is easy, because a water valve closes automatically as the tap body or outer cover is removed.

You'll find a small holding-nut at the top of a nozzle, which has to be unscrewed. Now turn the tap on and keep on turning, as if you were opening it. The water will flow and, at first, increase but suddenly the check-valve will be activated, stopping the flow of water. A few more turns of the nozzle and it will come off in your hand.

Hold the nozzle in your hand in its upright position and tap it on a hard surface (not on a breakable hand basin!). Now, turn it upside down and you'll find the anti-splash device, which holds the washer and the jumper inside it and which you'll see is finned, will fall out. Gently prise the washer and jumper from the end of the anti-splash device. You'll now see why this is one of the easiest of DIY problems to solve – the replacement simply presses into the finned device. To reassemble the tap is child's play!

## REPAIRING A LEAKING GLAND

At the top of the head-gear assembly is a spindle connected to the head of the tap. The head of the tap or handle is turned on and off to control the water supply. Because of this movement of a spindle in a static metal housing, somewhere in the assembly the spindle has to pass through a watertight but non-rigid material. This is the stuffing box or gland packing. It is simply a small hollow (or gland) into which specially impregnated hemp or twine is rammed tight. In old taps a packing can fail and will need to be replaced to prevent water dripping from under the head of the tap.

You don't have to turn off the stopcock (and the supply of water to the tap) to replace gland packing. Turn the tap off fully before removing the capstan head of the tap. A small grub-screw might be found at the side of the head holding it in position, or the holding-screw might be found underneath a small centre cover in the top of the capstan head. Lift off the head and cover and try the first remedy, which is to tighten a slack gland-nut. It often works but, if not, remove the nut with a spanner and pick out all remnants of the original packing. Wind the replacement packing around the spindle and force it tightly into the gland, with a small piece of wood. Reassemble the head-gear as before and once again check for leaks. If you should find a small rubber O ring instead of gland packing, it is likely that it has lost its resilience and needs to be replaced. O rings are as readily available as washers. Simply slip the ring over the spindle. It does the same job as the gland packing, preventing leaks through the head of the tap.

## MODERNIZING A TAP

If a tap is functioning well, there is no need to replace the whole thing when upgrading your bathroom. Special tap conversion-kits are available, in a number of colours and designs. Adaptors are designed for particular taps, so the one you choose will depend on the type of tap you have to convert.

Perhaps you replaced a tap washer and found that the tap was still dripping from the spout. This usually indicates that the seating is slightly worn or uneven and needs regrinding. One way to overcome this problem is to hire a special reseating-tool, but with the adaptor tap kit, this is no longer necessary! The replacement nylon seat will fit tightly into the existing worn seat with no need for regrinding.

Turn off the supply of water to the tap before removing the tap handle and head-gear mechanism. The boxed kit, to fit your particular tap, will have full instructions for this simple adaptation job.

## ICE-PLUGS AND BURST PIPES

Even though you feel that you've fully protected your house and the plumbing system against severe winter weather and frost, under certain conditions water pipes can still be vulnerable to frost and ice. Attics and lofts are the most likely place for bursts to occur because they are the coldest parts of the house.

## ICE-PLUGS

If your problem is lack of water when you turn on a hot tap then an ice-plug has probably formed in part of the hot water system. There is a risk of an explosion if it is allowed to go unchecked, and the immersion heater or boiler is not switched off – so switch it off immediately! Copper piping is an excellent conductor of heat, so apply some form of heat along the pipe away from the tap. Leave the tap open to encourage the flow of water when the plug of ice melts. The gentle use of a hot air gun or a hairdryer is recommended, but never a butane flame gun. The warmth will travel along the copper pipe some distance to melt the ice and clear the blockage. Leave the tap running for a while to warm up the whole length of the copper pipe. Try to find the source of the cold air and use an insulating material to prevent it happening again! Now switch the boiler and the immersion heater back on.

Quite often a waste pipe running through an external wall has its trap very close to the wall and this can form an ice-plug. A symptom of this is water not running away when it is freezing cold outside. Water remains in the U-bend of the trap as a seal to prevent foul smells entering the house from the sewage system. If it is left standing for a long time in the winter, it is very likely that it will freeze. Most traps and waste pipes nowadays are plastic and hot air or a naked flame will melt them. But the ice must be melted by the application of warmth. The problem is solved by wrapping hot towels around the trap and waste pipe. As soon as the towels cool replace immediately and repeat the procedure until the ice melts. As soon as the water flows from the basin, leave a hot tap running to warm up the rest of the waste system. To stop this recurring in cold conditions and especially if a sink or basin is infrequently used, add salt to the water in the trap. Check also that the waste pipe going through the exterior wall is completely sealed. If it isn't use a mastic sealant outside and inside to completely seal the joint.

## BURST PIPES

If you are unlucky enough to experience a burst pipe this is how to solve the problem. Don't rush to find the location of the burst but go immediately to the main stopcock and turn it off. If that is difficult, tie up the ball valve in the cold water storage tank. You simply lift the arm, which stops the flow of water into the tank, and tie it to a piece of wood laid across the top of the tank. Get everybody to turn on all the taps in the house and if one does not run then you've located an ice-plug position. Flush the WCs: if a cistern does not refill quickly the burst is in the supply pipe between the storage tank and that WC.

If water is dripping through a ceiling, take great care because it could have entered a junction box or a light fitting. Having turned off the taps to prevent serious flooding, there might still be a pool of water lying above a ceiling. You'll need to turn off the electricity supply before checking in the loft. Never use candles or matches in emergency but use your standby torch. In the room underneath the rapidly staining ceiling place a plastic sheet and buckets on the floor and poke a pointed stick through the centre of the wet patch. Once all the water has drained away, carry out a temporary repair.

Burst pipe repair kits are available at your DIY supercentre so buy a few different types and sizes to keep for an emergency. A steel clamp with a rubber gasket to seal over the split is a quick and efficient temporary repair aid; it is particularly useful because it can be used on different sizes of pipe, and re-used once the permanent repair has been carried out. Another useful emergency repair kit is a two-part resin sealant which sets rock hard around the split. Couplings are available, which are very easily inserted after the split part of the pipe has been cut out. If a joint has been affected by ice expansion it's probably not actually split but just pulled apart. Manufacturers have produced for the DIY market repair kits with compression joints and push-fit joints.

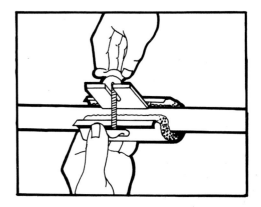

To effect a quick and efficient temporary repair to a burst pipe use either a resin-based two-part mix or a steel clamp (illustrated). This pipe clamp is readily available and should be kept handy in case of emergency. It can be used on different sizes of pipe and reused once the permanent repair has been carried out. The rubber gasket seals over the split in the pipe and the butterfly nut and bolt tightens the steel clamp to make a watertight repair.

# CHAPTER EIGHT

# HEATING, INSULATION AND VENTILATION

## RIDDING YOUR HOUSE OF MOULD

Inside our homes it is relative humidity that determines whether moulds grow, wood decays or decorations become spoiled. Sounds simple, and it is, but the development of these have an adverse effect not only on the structure of our homes but on our health too.

Outside the home, pollution is all around us. Sulphurs and pollutants in the air destroy our buildings and our health. Our temperate climate brings many advantages, but black mould, moss, fungi, lichen, algae and bacteria seem to thrive too when fed by the damp atmosphere and short bursts of sunshine.

Moulds, fungi and mites are the unwanted consequences of dampness, and condensation – which is practically pure water – provides a continuing source of food for the organisms. Dry up the source and the offenders will die. However, a certain amount of humidity is essential to our health and to the fabric of our homes so a balance has to be struck.

Stagnant, unmoving air can be contained in the corners of rooms that have cold external walls. This is because of lack of ventilation. Black moulds are often most severe there. Cupboards and wardrobes against external walls, particularly 9in (230mm) solid brick walls, provide ideal breeding grounds for moulds and mildew. Airborne spores fly in enormous numbers and variety all around us. Too small to see or feel, but feeding on moisture and tiny organic particles all the time, they result in mould and stains. These can be treated and eliminated, but the source of damp (condensation) must be remedied first. Fungicidal preparations with detergent properties can then be used leaving the surface free from contamination.

Condensation occurs when warm moist air meets a cold surface; for example, if you breathe on to a cold window your breath condenses and the result is water rivulets running down the window. A condensation level depends upon how moist the air is and the coldness of the surfaces of the building. Of course, both of these depend upon how the building is used, so get to the source of the problem first of all to prevent moist air spreading to other rooms from kitchens and bathrooms. Provide ventilation to all rooms and use heating sensibly. Cooking potatoes in the kitchen produces an enormous amount of moisture. If the kitchen door is left open, that moisture permeates to the rest of the house. The secret is to leave windows open (or to have an electric extractor fan working) but to keep doors closed. Some parents tell their children, 'after a bath, open the door, don't let the bathroom steam up!' It's a mistake. A shout goes to the person who is drying clothes, 'leave the door open, the room is steaming up!' That too produces condensation and damp problems throughout the house.

In older houses ventilation occurs naturally through fireplace flues and draughty windows. It's uncomfortable in cold weather to have too much ventilation and it also wastes heat, but some ventilation is absolutely essential both for the fabric of your house and for your health. Modern flats with double glazing and houses with up-to-date improvements of complete draught proofing will certainly not have sufficient ventilation. Ventilation is essential for a reasonable time each day throughout your home and nearly all the time that a room is in use.

It has been worked out scientifically that condensation is produced in frightening amounts when a portable paraffin or flueless gas heater is used. For each litre of oil used, the equivalent of about a litre of liquid water in the form of water vapour is produced. Airing cupboards are a mistake, unless they are properly ventilated. Homes left unoccupied and unheated during the day get very cold. If possible it really is best to keep some heating on, even at the lowest level. It takes a long time for floors and particularly walls to warm up, so remember that it's better to have a small amount of heat on for a long period than to have shorts bursts of full heat. In bungalows and flats that have a lot of outside wall area, condensation is a very likely hazard. It's very useful to have an inexpensive thermometer to check temperature levels in various rooms. Even if your home is well insulated and has reasonable ventilation it's necessary to maintain all rooms at not less than 50°F (10°C) during cold weather in order to avoid condensation. However, when rooms are in use their temperature should be about 68°F (20°C). If you spot any sign of mould growth, a condensation problem has to be solved. Heating, structural insulation, ventilation or all three will need your DIY expertise.

New building work of brick, stone and especially plaster takes a long time to dry out completely. Extra heat and ventilation is called for during this time. In a room that has been newly plastered, make use of a hired dehumidifier. Condensation and moisture is extracted from the room and converted to water. This water is discharged through the machine into a bucket and you'll be amazed at how quickly that bucket will be filled! If any of your rooms has a gas or solid fuel appliance a constant air supply is essential. If you propose to fit an extractor fan, or to change the ventilation in that room in any way at all, obtain advice from a professional – the Gas Board or the Solid Fuel Advisory Service – about the risks of drawing toxic fumes back into the room.

## CLEARING INTERIOR MOULD

A powerful fungicidal solution, preferably with detergent properties, is needed to clear black mould, mildew and other fungi from interior surfaces to leave them clean and free from contamination. One such product called Mould Buster has recently been tested by the Department of Environment Research Establishment and is available in DIY outlets. For hard and nonporous surfaces such as tiles, use a clean cloth well damped with fungicidal wash to wipe away all traces of mould. Continue the cleaning and rinsing process working in an area of about a square yard (square metre) at a time. Finally, leave a film of the fungicidal solution on the surface to protect against recontamination. Allow this film to dry overnight. The instructions on the container will tell you that it is not a primary skin irritant but sensible precautions must be taken during use.

Mould on wallpaper can be treated by applying a low-cost acrylic clear emulsion which can be used on most wallpapers to cure mould growth. It dries in just two hours to a clear, semi-matt, colourless film. It will also give long-term protection against further mould attack and can be used as a fungicidal sealer prior to any wallpapering.

This clear emulsion, properly prepared and applied, is durable and fully washable so can be applied to most surfaces to give protection. You can even use it outside your house, to clean and protect exterior decorations in areas worst affected by mould and growth.

## CLEARING EXTERIOR MOULD

To restore existing exterior decorations, carefully clean the surface with fungicidal wash, allow it to dry then apply one or two thin coats of acrylic clear emulsion with a clean brush. Depending on ambient temperatures, in good conditions the film should be dry for recoating in two to four hours. It can be used quite safely in all areas where circumstances require a non-toxic coating.

To treat exterior walls of brick, stone, stucco and render, as well as patios of natural or made-up slabs, paths or even cobble stones, use a powerful fungicidal wash concentrate. Dilute 1½ pints (1 litre) of the wash concentrate with 7 pints (4 litres) of water and thoroughly soak the area to be treated, as your last job one evening. There is no rubbing or scrubbing, in fact while you are sleeping your patio or wall is undergoing a cleaning and protection process! All that is left for you to do is to remove the dead growth in the morning. For all jobs of this nature it is a sensible precaution to wear gloves and wellington boots.

## SOUND INSULATION

We live in a noisy world. More often than not the sound levels are not ours to control and we often have to suffer unnecessary noise. In our homes though it should be different. When we need to relax and be quiet we should be able to. Unfortunately, it isn't always so.

Thoughtfully designed buildings, whether single- or multiple-occupation, in theory should have no acoustic problems. Building Regulations ensure that adequate density is provided in the structure to offset the risk of transmission of sound through walls and floors in multi-occupied buildings. Often though we are made to suffer the results of cheapness and poor workmanship in blocks of flats and hotels.

The consequences of low standards of conversions of large houses in this country have been suffered by millions of people. Where the houses have been subdivided horizontally or vertically into separate dwellings, very little thought has been given to insulating walls and floors. Developers often overlook or disregard the need to achieve a prescribed level of sound insulation during conversion work. Two different forms of noise transmission have to be prevented – impact noise as created by footsteps or hammering on a wall and airborne sound as produced by voices, television, etc. During building work it is quite easy to install materials of high density to create a noise barrier. But of course it costs the developer time and money. It is easier and cheaper to disregard the problem because the materials are hidden anyway.

Manufacturers are aware of this basic need of ours to enjoy peace and quiet in our own homes. Products have been designed for the DIY enthusiast to reduce sound transmission from one dwelling to another.

The best sound insulator is the densest material. Victorian builders used sheet lead on the floors of bathrooms and toilets located over sitting rooms. Nobody ever complained of noise! It is one of the best sound insulators known to man. Rarely do flat conversions enjoy the benefits afforded by this expensive material.

The floor construction of larger properties converted to flats is usually of timber joists to which floorboards are nailed above and plasterboards to the ceiling below, so that the density between the two neighbouring flats might be only ¾in (20mm) of floorboard and ⅝in (16mm) of ceiling board, or lath and plaster. On a scale of 1 to 10 for sound insulation this type of construction rates only 4, or even less if there are gaps in floorboards! Direct air gaps and air paths, such as ill-fitting skirting boards, gaps around windows and doors, ventilators and air bricks, allow even more sound through. It is important to understand that the tiniest hairline crack between a wall and ceiling in an otherwise high-density material will allow you to identify whispers in an adjacent flat. Installing sound insulation material is fairly easy; however, it is imperative that no gaps or cracks are overlooked or neglected.

## SOUND INSULATION BETWEEN FLOORS

Sound insulation between floors can be achieved in one of three ways: a new floor isolated from the original structure can be installed; a newly-designed system can be installed underneath the original floorboards; or a false ceiling, totally independent from the existing can be built. Once you've begun to appreciate what causes sound problems you'll be nearer to understanding how to solve them.

Sound engineers in radio know about a phenomenon which they can sometimes exploit but, to the flat-dweller suffering this particular problem, it is no joke! Thin barriers of building materials can actually increase the intensity of sound on the other side, as happens when sound waves, either impact or airborne, hit the floor and cause reverberations (intensified sound). Neighbours living above you with no carpet on the floor, a television playing in the night or a barking dog give cause for concern. The neighbour above you could, of course, be suffering your noises too! This is a direct result of lack of knowledge or neglect by the builder. It's worth noting that good sound absorption can be provided by furnishings such as curtains and carpets which prevent sound leaving a room.

Ideally, it is easier to insulate from the floor above to effectively reduce airborne and impact noises passing either way. Lift the floorboards and lay a sound absorbing material between the joists, cutting out all air gaps around the walls too. Take care when handling cables and pipes. When replacing the floorboards squeeze three or four boards together using a well-tried DIY method with wedges. (*See* section on replacing damaged floorboards, p.53.) As you proceed with the laying of the boards mark the exact positions of cables and pipes on top of the boards with a felt pen. These marks must be transferred to the top layer of insulating material so that no pipes or cables are pierced by floor nails in the future.

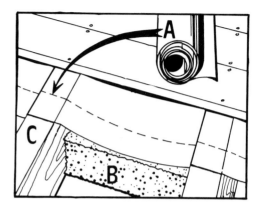

Specially-made, thinly-rolled, lead-based sound insulation material (**A**) is laid directly on to the joists, after a layer of 4in (100mm) Gyplas (**B**) is sandwiched between the joists (**C**). The floorboards are fixed in the normal way with no loss of sound insulation. Ensure that the boards are firmly tightened to each other using a clamp or wedges. Overlap the sheet lead by at least 3in (75mm) and use a flexible mastic sealant on the lap.

½in (12mm) thick insulating board is now laid and fixed on to the floorboards and then covered with hardboard. Tiles or underlay and carpet would complete a very good sound barrier. The doors of the room will have to be adjusted. (*See* p.84) Alternatively, a sheet of thin-gauge lead could be laid on the joists. This gives an incredibly dense form of insulation but pieces must be overlapped to provide a continuous sheet with no gaps especially at the walls.

The second method of dealing with the floor is to use a new Gyproc product. In tests it has proved to be very effective as a sound barrier, without the disadvantage of raising the floor by inches. In fact the system adds

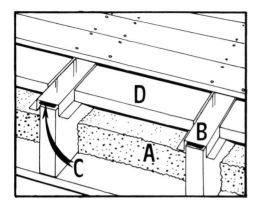

and, properly carried out, creates an effective sound barrier.

The third method to reduce sound levels from a room or flat above is to erect a totally independent ceiling below the existing ceiling. Sometimes this isn't possible due to limited ceiling height or if windows and doors are very close to existing ceilings. A minimum of 6in (150mm) is recommended between the two ceilings. Installing an independent ceiling is fairly easy but if major structural alterations or changes to the

Gyplas, 4in (100mm) glass wool mat (**A**), is laid between the joists with no gaps. Metal channel sections (**B**) are laid on the joists. Resilient strips (**C**) are located between the metal channel and the joists. ¾in (19mm) Gyproc plank (**D**) is cut and fitted to rest on the metal flanges. The floor is completed by screwing the floorboards through the plank into the metal flanges.

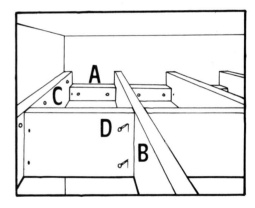

only a ¼in (6mm) to the height of the floor. After lifting the floorboards 4in (100mm) of insulation material is laid between each joist, tight to the sides. 1½in (35mm) clips are then attached at regular intervals along the joists. Aluminium flanges, incorporating a ¼in (6mm) strip of special foam, run along each joist. A sound insulating board is then dropped on to the flanges, between the joists. New floor decking, or the old floorboards, are then laid on top of the aluminium flanges. The floor is fixed to the aluminium flange, but effectively floats above the joists, isolated on the strip of foam. The resilient foam strips are pre-fitted into the metal 'top hat' section. This system has been designed for the enthusiastic DIYer

If only the underside of a separating floor is accessible, construct an independent ceiling. Drill, plug and screw 2 × 2in (50 × 50mm) battens (**A**) at least 6in (150mm) below the existing ceiling on the end walls to level lines. These will support notched joists (**B**), skew nailed to the battens. The side joists (**C**) are fixed to the walls with plugs and screws. Intermediate noggings (**D**) are skew nailed to support the ends of the plasterboards. The lower edges of all joists, battens and noggings must be level to take the plasterboards. Lay mineral fibre insulation between the timbers before fixing the plasterboards.

electrical services are involved seek the advice of a professional.

The new ceiling will be formed by constructing a framework of timber battens to which two layers of plasterboard are fixed. Glass fibre or mineral wool is laid either between or above the new joists to provide a continuous blanket. 2in × 2in (50mm × 50mm) battens are levelled and screwed to the side walls. 6in × 1½in (150mm × 35mm) battens are notched and skew-nailed in position to support the edges of the plasterboard. (*See* illustration on p.107, and right.) Use nonrust screws and a powered screw driver, to save on arm-ache and disturbance by banging nails with a hammer! The first layer of plasterboard is butt-jointed, but the second layer should be taper-edged. A kit is available which includes filler, tapes and tools, to give a smooth flush finish to the joints. The plasterboard ceiling can then be papered or painted. Make certain that all wall-to-ceiling joints are completely filled, with no air gaps to spoil the insulation treatment.

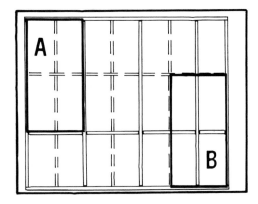

Illustration shows a typical layout of timbers for a 14ft × 12ft (4.25 × 3.6m) bedroom ceiling. The solid lines indicate the supporting timbers for the first layer of plasterboards. Plasterboard (**A**) is fixed first. The dotted lines show the fixing positions for the second layer of plasterboards, ensuring that no joints coincide. Plasterboard (**B**) is the first one to be fixed of the second layer. Fix each layer into all intermediate timbers too.

When the ceiling is finished, fit coving to be certain that no sound can escape around the ceiling/wall joint.

## SOUND INSULATION BETWEEN WALLS

Walls with noise problems can also be dealt with effectively. Check the construction of the wall first. Find out whether floorboards run through from one room to the next. If there is an attic above, does the offending wall continue up to underneath the roof covering? If not, is the floor of the attic insulated in any way? If the wall is of stud-type construction, the performance of sound insulation can be improved by removing the plasterboard and filling the cavity with Gypglas–1000 before replacing the plaster-

board facing. Further improvement can be achieved by nailing an additional layer of plasterboard to one or both sides. Stagger the joints of the second layer of plasterboard and remember to fill every gap.

If there is room to reduce the floor area by 9in (230mm) along the wall, a more effective method is to build another stud partition wall. This new wall should be isolated from the original with a gap of at least 4in (100mm). Use 4in × 2in (100mm × 50mm) sawn timbers, fix a sole plate to the floor and

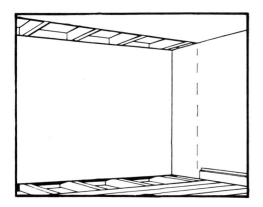

Remove skirting boards (to be re-used), cut away plasterboard and lift floorboards. Fill between joists with Gypglas insulating material as far as you can, filling every gap.

Seek professional advice if electrical or plumbing services are to be moved. Fix timbers to ceiling and floor joists and to a vertical line on each wall for the outer framework of the new stud wall.

Mineral wool multi-purpose slabs are ideal for in-filling between studs as acoustic insulation. If the studs and noggings are fixed directly to a solid wall simply cut the slabs to size and press against the brickwork. Otherwise use a plastic mesh stapled to the back of the timbers to prevent the slabs falling into the void. Use gloves and protective clothing. Finish by fixing two layers of plasterboard, without joints coinciding.

a header vertically above it to the ceiling. At intervals of 16in (400mm) fix upright studs. In between the upright studs fix short horizontal pieces of 4in × 2in (100mm × 50mm) timbers (called noggings), to stabilize the structure and to support the edges of the plasterboard. Staple plastic netting to the back edges of the structure to support and prevent the Gypglas-1000 from falling into the gap. Use galvanized plasterboard nails to fix two layers of plasterboard to the face of the stud partition wall. Remember to stagger and fill the joints to make a smooth finish to take either wallpaper or paint.

An easier method, which will reduce the size of your room less, is to fix directly to

the wall an insulating board specially designed for this purpose. The sandwich is made up of dense plasterboard and highly compressed polystyrene. It is easily sawn and lightweight to handle. Blobs of plaster or special adhesive can be used to fix it to the original wall. The decorative side will take any wall covering or paint.

Open fireplaces can create problems of noise between dwellings. Sometimes as little as 4½in (115mm) of brick separates one fireplace from another backing on to it. If the fireplace is not in use and there are problems of noise intrusion, consider blocking it up. If the fireplace is used during the winter months only then it might be worth constructing a temporary frame and a cover board. If a chimney flue is deprived of a current of air, the result will be condensation and its attendant problems within the flue. So it is essential to install a vent.

A solid wall, either brick or block, is denser and therefore has better sound insulating qualities than a stud wall. If there is a requirement for better sound insulation in a basement, or a ground floor having a solid concrete floor, then a separate solid wall will solve that problem. Ensure that the base is at least 4in (100mm) of concrete. If the walls either side are solid, use angled metal wall ties to firmly anchor the new wall. If the ceiling is of solid construction build tightly to it. A plasterboard ceiling though needs some extra work! If the ceiling joists are at right angles to the new wall, remove a strip of plasterboard above the wall. Stuff plenty of insulating material into the gaps before screwing a 4in × 2in (100mm × 50mm) timber (a header), to the joists immediately above the wall. Build up the solid wall tight to the header. Force pieces of slate into the gap before pointing with mortar. If the joists run parallel to the new wall build up as high as possible between the joists. Insulate all gaps in the ceiling void as far as you can. Fix a batten to the new wall,

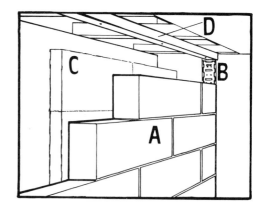

For best results on a solid concrete floor construct a wall of acoustic building blocks (**A**). Metal crocodile stainless steel wall plates (**B**) make it easy to fix the new wall to the solid side walls. Between the existing wall and the new one, fit slabs of mineral wool (**C**) taking them tight to and into the ceiling void. Fill every cavity as far as possible in the ceiling. Build the blockwork wall tight to the new header timber (**D**) fixed to the underside of the joists.

so that it's in line with the bottom of the existing joists and make good the ceiling. Press a layer of plasterboard into blobs of plaster on the new wall and you'll not only get further insulation, but a very good surface to take your final decorations!

## REMOVING A RADIATOR

There are a number of reasons why a radiator might have to be removed. You might, for example, feel cheated if you couldn't get a professional finish by wallpapering behind the radiator! To seal and paint the back or even replace a radiator necessitates a lift-off. And surprisingly, in most cases it is not necessary to drain the system in order to lift off a radiator. The proviso is that there is a valve either side of the radiator, a locked valve on the one side and control valve on the other. (Incidentally, it is important to drain out the water if the house is left unattended for a length of time in the winter.)

A radiator of average size can be removed by one person in less than an hour by following these step-by-step instructions. Obviously it's easier and quicker with a helper, especially if you're going to find sludge in the bottom of the radiator! But more about that later. By closing both valves it's possible to undo the compression joints and lift the radiator off its brackets

## PREPARATION

Now, as with all DIY jobs, procedure in the correct order is important, so start by laying a plastic sheet covered with a dust sheet underneath the radiator. You'll need a screwdriver, shifting spanners and some water containers. A couple of square ice-cream tubs are ideal for this job. If the central heating system has been in use, cool the radiator by closing the control valve. There's bound to be some spillage of dirty water so have lots of rags nearby. You'll need one or two buckets as well as the ice-cream containers, which will fit underneath the lower joints of the radiator, to catch the draining water.

## DRAINING THE RADIATOR

First close the control valve by turning the plastic control wheel clockwise. The central holding screw can then be released to lift off the control wheel. The plastic cover on the locking valve at the other end of the radiator can now be pulled off and the control wheel pushed on in its place. Use it to turn off the locking valve. It's important to count the number of turns required to close the locking valve. The same number of reverse turns will be needed to open it later on because the radiator was at one time correctly balanced and it needs to be set again. A pipe wrench or an adjustable spanner can be used to gently turn the large compression nut holding the control valve to the radiator. Once you've opened the vent at the top of the radiator with the special square key, water will begin to drain off. You can now actually control the flow of water by opening and closing the vent. Prop something under-neath the radiator to support the valve and copper pipe to prevent distortion. Other-wise your able helper can do this! It doesn't take long for the water to drain off. Leave the vent open and when the water has stopped running, turn your attention to the valve at the other end of the radiator. This is the locked valve. Release the compression nut completely. Some water might still flow out, so be ready with your containers.

With the radiator still supported, dis-connect the control valve completely and spring out the valves from the radiator to lift it off its brackets. You'll need to be very quick with the rags because you have to cover both holes whilst carrying the radiator outside. Take great care because that sludge can permanently stain a carpet! With a hose pipe in one end and the outlet over a gully, flush it out until clear water runs. If a great deal of black sludge is present ask at your

DIY supercentre for a corrosion inhibitor. Full instructions on introducing this into the system are supplied with it and any chemical corrosion-proofer which might be necessary.

If you need to remove the brackets to wallpaper, pop matchsticks in to the plugs in the wall. These will pierce the new wallpaper making it easy to locate the brackets again.

## REFITTING THE RADIATOR

To refit the radiator first clean out the couplings in the valves and on the radiator to remove any debris that might be left behind. Gently lift the radiator back onto the refitted brackets and check with your partner that it is sitting properly and the valves are exactly in line with the compression joints. Tighten each nut by hand, then use an adjustable spanner. Remember at all times to support the valves and pipework as if it is not in line you could end up with leaks. Now open the control valve which allows the radiator to fill. Open the vent a little and you can hear air being expelled as the radiator fills. It's best to hold a rag to the vent until the air is expelled and a little water is seen. Close the vent and open the locked valve to get the warm water circulating. Have you remembered about the number of turns? Well, look at your notes and open with the same number of turns used to close it previously! A simply DIY test for leaks – hold a finger against the joints and if there's any trace of water on your finger tips, gently tighten the compression nuts. Check again. No glisten means no leaks!

## COMMON PROBLEMS IN GAS- OR OIL-FIRED CENTRAL HEATING SYSTEMS
## HOT RADIATORS WITH COOL AREAS

A cool patch in the centre of a radiator whilst the top and/or ends are warm can only happen in a system that has been running for some time. A chemical reaction takes place within the system between the water, copper pipework and steel radiators. This produces deposits of corrosion at the bottom of radiators in the form of a black sludge. The longer the system has been running with no protection from corrosion, the heavier the deposits will be. And the circulation of water in the radiators is restricted which in turn produces the cool and warm patches. This is a problem that can be solved by introducing a proprietary corrosion inhibitor to the water. Do it as soon as you spot the symptom because if it is allowed to build up, the sludge can clog the pump and reduce the heat output of radiators by partially blocking them.

When a central heating system is first installed, an inhibitor should be introduced following the manufacturer's instructions. It is so simple to do at that stage, by pouring the liquid into the water tank and allowing it to circulate into the system. However, it is never too late to overcome this problem provided the system is operating.

Refer now to the section Fitting Radiator Thermostats on page 115. Read the paragraph that tells you how to drain the system. If your central heating system has been running for sometime and you are experiencing problems of cool patches in radiators then it is better to flush out the entire system by draining and refilling repeatedly until the water runs clean from the hose into the gully. If the problem is slight and only one radiator has been affected then all you need do is drain off enough water to empty the feed and expansion tank and some water from the pipework. About 5 gallons (23 litres) is enough to drain off. The manufacturer's instructions will tell you to pour the inhibitor into the tank and to restore the water supply. In most cases the instructions will say that about 1 gallon (5 litres) is enough for most systems. But as you'll see from the manufacturer's instructions the amount will depend upon the size of the boiler and of your system.

By switching on the circulating pump the inhibitor is going to be distributed right round the system through the pipework and the radiators. The protection process has commenced! It is now worth going round each radiator in turn checking that there is no air left in the radiators by using the vent key and that there are no leaks anywhere. If there are, make the necessary adjustments and once again check that the draincocks are closed.

## BANGING SOUNDS IN THE SYSTEM OR BOILER

Some problems of banging in an overworked system can be analysed and solved by sharing the work with the engineer who does your annual service. However, the most likely fault is lack of water in the central heating system, and this problem can very easily be analysed and solved without calling in the engineer. First of all, shut down the boiler and check the feed and expansion tank in the attic. The level of water must be maintained just below the overflow pipe. In the tank is a ball float-arm and valve. As the water lowers, the arm opens the valve and water flows into the tank. If the tank is empty it could be that the valve is stuck. By moving the arm up and down you should be able to restore the flow of water and refill the tank. If you don't get a supply of water check that the mains water has not been turned off and left off, either at the main stopcock or the one controlling the supply to the tank. The worst time that this could happen, of course, is in the winter when you need heat most. So perhaps the supply pipe is frozen. Make a thorough investigation and warm up what might be an ice-plug in part of the rising main. If a split has already appeared buy a simple two-part repair kit or a pipe-clamp to overcome the problem.

The two other reasons for banging sounds in the boiler or pipework are either scale deposits in the system due to very hard water or perhaps a faulty boiler thermostat.

A simple inexpensive test kit will tell you what degree of hardness you have in your mains water supply. If you live in a hard water area it is advisable to have a descaler introduced into the system when your service engineer next carries out his annual inspection. Most of the work involved is draining, flushing and refilling the system, which is covered in Chapter 7 and easy enough for most householders.

To check for a faulty boiler thermostat, which could be the cause of banging sounds in the boiler, first shut down the boiler. Don't switch off the pump because you need the water to circulate around the system in order to cool quickly. When the water is sufficiently cool it is possible to operate the boiler thermostat control by hand, until you hear a clicking sound. Every boiler has a manual supplied with full instructions and information on separate controls. Refer to the section covering operation of thermostat. Listen for the clicking sound, but if there is none, then and only then do you have to refer to your engineer. When you make your telephone call tell him the make of boiler and the capacity. Then surprise him by saying that you've diagnosed the problem as being a faulty boiler thermostat because you can hear no clicking when you operate the control! His visit will be a very short one because the fitting is a very simple operation.

## SINGLE RADIATOR REMAINING COLD

Make the simpler checks first, before checking for inlet or outlet valves blocked up by black sludge. Your first simple check is the inlet valve. Is the supply pipe just below the valve hot? It probably is and therefore the fault could be in the valve itself. If it's an older type manual inlet valve and not a thermostatic valve then the valve could be closed. Check the setting of the valve and open it if that is necessary. If a thermostatic valve is fitted check that it is set properly. If not, open it up to its maximum setting. If still no hot water flows through, the valve is faulty and has to be replaced. Check your guarantee date. Unfortunately to replace one faulty valve means that the system has to be drained down. (*See* Chapter 7)

The lockshield valve at the other end of the radiator has to be properly balanced when the system is serviced. If for some reason the lockshield cover has been moved and the setting altered this naturally affects the heat output of the radiator. It is a simple matter to remove the cover and open the setting to its maximum to find out if it affects the performance of the radiator. If it does not, return to the original setting – and now check for corrosion.

By closing both valves and unscrewing the compression nuts holding the valves to the radiator it is a simple job for two people to lift off the radiator. (But first refer to the section on p.110 on removing a radiator.) To flush out one single radiator the system does not have to be drained down, so it is not a very time consuming job. To carry the radiator outside, close the air vent, hold rags over the inlet and outlet openings and turn the radiator upside down. There'll be a certain amount of spillage, but as long as you've protected floor coverings with a sheet of plastic then the black sludge cannot harm your carpet. Run a hose into the radiator and over a drain. Wait until you have clean water coming out the other end before replacing it.

## COOL TOP ON A RADIATOR

This problem is caused by an air lock at the top of the radiator. Hot water is circulating successfully in the rest of the radiator but prevented from reaching the top because of trapped air. This is the easiest problem to overcome in a central heating system: simply release the air with the aid of the vent key until water appears, then close the valve.

In a central heating system that has been running for some years air is not the only cause of locks in radiators. All central heating systems are made of materials that can become corroded. Pressed-steel radiators used in conjuction with copper tubing and water produce an electrolytic corrosion which results in sludge and 'air' in the system, this air is actually hydrogen gas, not dangerous but still able to cause an air lock. To check whether corrosion is taking place you can carry out a very simple test. Before you begin remove curtains and other inflammable materials close by. Take normal precautions and then it is quite safe. Have a lighted taper at the ready, open the air vent and bring the lighted taper to the escaping gas. If it burns with a blue flame hydrogen is certainly present, indicating that you have probably got corrosion. No blue flame means it is a straightforward air lock solved once again with the vent key.

Sometimes a vent valve becomes jammed. One of the reasons for this is because the wrong sized key is being used. In most households small keys like these are kept in kitchen drawers and they often get lost. These inexpensive keys are available at any DIY store, so take an impression of the plug using plasticine so that you get exactly the size key to fit your radiators. Buy a spare one while you're at it, it's worth it. If a build-up of paint is the problem, use a paint stripper to unjam it. Use only sufficient to release the threads and neutralize the stripper afterwards with either water or white spirit, as recommended by the makers.

## FITTING RADIATOR THERMOSTATS

Nearly 70 per cent of the homes in the UK are owner occupied and the majority have a central heating system. Therefore a high percentage of home owners are likely to be confronted with a central heating problem which can be solved by a competent DIYer. The common faults that occur in a gas- or oil-fired central heating system should not require the services of an engineer to put them right. We all know and appreciate the comfort that a central heating system affords. We should also be fully aware of how the system operates.

When it is needed water is heated in the boiler, flows around the system through the radiators and returns to the boiler to be re-heated. A small, silent electric pump ensures that the water continues to flow steadily and evenly. An electrically-controlled room thermostat senses the temperature of the room or hall and controls the output of heat in the system.

Each central heating system has to be separately designed. A heating engineer has to take into account the heating needs of each part of the house and the rate at which heat is lost. Obviously the construction of the walls, floors and ceilings are important factors. Insulation is another important factor. The temperature to which each part of the house is to be heated must be taken into account. The standard temperature for a living- or dining-room is 70°F (21°C); kitchen, hall and landing 60 to 65°F (15 to 19°C); bathroom 72°F (23°C) and bedrooms 60°F (15°C). Sizes of radiators and boiler are then determined. The two main systems in common use are the one-pipe system and the two-pipe system. In the single-pipe system water flows from the boiler through one

pipe only and back to the boiler to be reheated. On its way around the pipe the hot water is diverted into and out from radiators. In theory the last radiator in the circuit is going to be cooler but there are sophisticated controls which can be installed in the system to alleviate this problem. The two-pipe system has a flow pipe from the boiler taking the hot water to the radiators. A separate return pipe takes the cooled water from each radiator back to the boiler.

High technology in controls by way of thermostats, zone controllers and programmers means that you have a higher

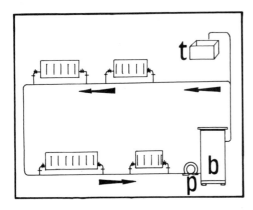

A one-pipe 'wet' central heating system showing direction of flow of hot water from boiler (**b**). The pump (**p**) can be located either side of the boiler but the feed pipe must also continue up over the tank (**t**) to discharge any hot water that builds up excessively. This is the safety factor in this type of system where a vent pipe is open to discharge expansion of hot water due to overheating. Note that the flow and return pipes of each radiator are connected to the same pipe, hence 'one-pipe system'.

Water is heated in the boiler (**b**), forced by the pump (**p**) through the pipes to all the radiators warming each room before it is returned to the boiler for re-heating. The tank (**t**) keeps the system topped up and safely takes any expansion of water through the open vent pipe that may result due to overheating.

Note that the hot water flows along one pipe and into each radiator but is returned to be reheated through a separate pipe, hence 'two-pipe system'.

level of automatic control over where you want the heat and when. Unfortunately, many central heating systems were installed with just one room thermostat, usually located in the hall. This meant that there was no separate control on individual radiators. To suit our own special needs, it is sometimes necessary to lower the heat in one room whilst boosting it, perhaps because of illness, in a bedroom. Now, with little expertise, step-by-step guidance and an inexpensive Thermostatic Radiator Valve (TRV) this problem is easily solved! This is one of the easiest of DIY jobs because no solder or heat is necessary, only spanners for the com-

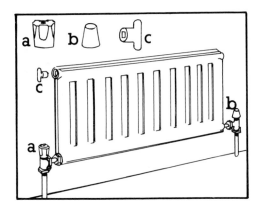

The control wheel (a) opens and closes the control valve at the inlet side of the radiator. The plastic cover (b) on the locking valve can be pulled off so that the control wheel can be used to open or close the locking valve. Air can be released from a radiator by opening the bleed valve at the top with the special radiator key (c). If part of a radiator is cold, it is probably due to an air pocket which can be dispersed through the bleed valve with the key.

pression joints. The thermostatic valve must be fitted to the inlet or flow side of the radiator. But how does one check this? Check by turning on the radiator from cold to find out which pipe gets warm first. Simple isn't it? Most radiators are fitted with two valves, called a hand wheel or control valve and a locked valve or locked shield valve. At the top of the radiator is a vent valve which can be opened to release air trapped in the system.

Before fitting a TRV, there are a few checks to be made. Is it a one- or two-pipe central heating system? This affects the choice of TRV. Most heating systems are now two-pipe, but the way to check is to lift a couple of floorboards in the bedroom underneath the radiator. At the same time check the size of the pipework; it is probably standard ½in (12mm). If you choose to fit TRVs on every radiator, it's worth checking them all at the same time and marking the inlet valve on each radiator. It is often the side with the 'On' and 'Off' turning wheel but it is not always the case so you should do the warm pipe test.

Now turn off the central heating system because you will need to drain it down. Look for the drainage valve which is located at the lowest point in the system. It's just like a small spout of a tap with a nut which can be opened with a spanner to allow the water to flow out. Attach a hose pipe to the valve with a jubilee clip and run the hose to an outside drain or gully. To stop the system refilling from the expansion tank, turn off the stopcock or tie up the ballcock so that it won't drop with the water level. Before opening the draincock allow the water in the system to cool. Having switched off the

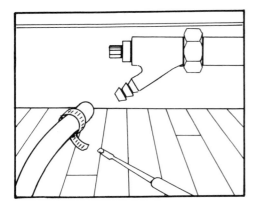

After the system has cooled down, switch off the pump and turn off the water supply to the feed and expansion tank. Now drain the system. The main draincock will be found at the lowest point near the boiler. Tighten one end of a garden hose onto the outlet of the draincock and run the other end to a gully outside. Open the draincock with the special key or a wrench. As the water runs away, open each of the radiator bleed valves starting at the top of the house to release a vacuum which could hold water in the radiators.

pump and turned off the mains water supply to the feed and expansion tank in the attic, you are ready to open the draincock. A key should be supplied for the square shank on the draincock or you can use an adjustable spanner.

If you suck water into a straw and put your finger over the top of the straw, the water will be held by vacuum and will not flow through the open bottom end. Sometimes a vacuum can form in a radiator in your central heating system too. To break the vacuum, allow air to enter the tops of each radiator by carefully opening the radi-ator bleed valves. Start at the top of the house. As you work downwards in the system, opening each of the air-vent valves (bleed valves), allow time for the water to drain away. Check outside at the gully when the water has stopped flowing.

In some houses with solid concrete floors, it might have been necessary to loop pipe runs up and over door openings creating what are called 'inverted pipe-loops'. Because of this, each pipeloop will have its own draincock. These must be drained separately after the water has stopped flowing from the main system.

You will need to choose the TRV to suit your particular system. Check whether it's a

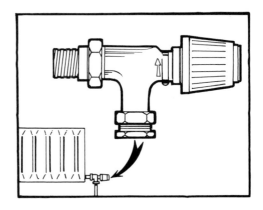

Thermostatically controlled radiator valves must be fitted to the flow connection only. To check this, turn all radiators off to start system from cold. Turn each radiator on and note which connection warms first. This will be the flow pipe. These thermostatic valves automatically and reliably keep room temperatures to the level that is pre-set. They prevent overheating of the room and save fuel.

one-pipe or two-pipe system and the size of pipe, before reading the illustrated leaflet from your DIY store. Now comes the interesting part – fitting the thermostatic valve. Inside the package you'll find manufacturer's illustrated instructions for fitting. In simple terms, the control valve is removed and the TRV fitted in its place. By undoing two compression nuts it's very simple to lift off the valve. Force will not be necessary but do support the pipework so that there is no risk of joints being forced apart below the floorboards. A small threaded joint is now left in the radiator. It is called a union tail and must be removed and replaced by the one in the package. A spanner with a square shank or the squared end of a pliers handle can be used to unscrew the union tail. Replace it with the new tail which is part of the TRV kit. Before fitting, wind on to the thread some plumbers' joint sealing tape, called PTFE tape, running in the same direction as the thread. This helps to make a watertight seal. As part of the compression joint on the original control valve, you'll see a tight copper ring left on the pipe itself. The instructions will ask you to cut the pipe just below that ring or 'olive' and clean up the pipe, especially of paint. Drop the new nut over the pipe, then the new 'olive' and smear a sealing compound around it.

Now the new valve can be very simply fitted in place. Don't over-tighten the nuts because any leaks encountered when the system is refilled can be overcome by tightening them further. Remove the green cap, but keep it safe to shut off the radiator fully in the future. You'll find a sensor which simply pushes on to the valve body; make

sure that the marker points upwards, then just tighten the adjusting band.

Having accomplished what might have seemed a daunting task, sit down, have a drink and go through the instruction leaflet again. You'll now more fully understand the fitting of the TRV. This will make the installation of the rest of the TRVs simpler and certainly more satisfying. When you've finished take away the hose pipe and close the draincock and, in sequence, go to each radiator and check that you've tightened all the nuts and closed each air vent valve. Now restore the water supply to the feed and expansion tank in the attic. As the radiators fill up, air will be held trapped in the tops. Wait until the water stops running and then starting at the bottom of the house, open the air vent valve in each radiator in turn. Hold a rag against the valve key; when all the air has escaped and signs of water appear, close the valve.

Allow the system to warm up before making your final checks of all draincocks and air vent valves for signs of leakage. Gently tighten where necessary. A simple but very effective test is to put your finger underneath the joint and if there is a leak the tip of your finger will glisten. Leave the pump running for a while before checking that all the radiators are warming up.

Having had the system drained down and air drawn inevitably into the system, there is a very slight possibility that an airlock might have formed in the pump. The symptom is that even though the pump is running, the radiators don't seem to be warming up. You solve this problem very simply with a screwdriver or a vent key. The pump is located next to the boiler. On the side of the pump is an air vent valve specially for this purpose. It will be marked. Switch the pump off before you open the valve. Be prepared for a slight spillage of water after the air has escaped, then fully close the valve. Switch on the pump and the problem should be solved.

Now you have full control of every radiator in each separate location to add to everybody's comfort in the home! The thermostats automatically and reliably keep the room temperatures to the level of comfort that each individual wants. They are entirely independent of changes in weather conditions and changes of conditions within the house itself. A simple adjustment of the easily read calibrations on the thermostat will allow a change of setting and temperature in any room.

The fitting of radiator thermostats has yet another advantage. The Department of Energy recommends that you fit heating controls to radiators to save fuel and to bring your heating system under total control. It is claimed that each 1°C reduction of the temperature of the home will take eight per cent off the heating bill! Radiator thermostats also prevent overheating by automatically regulating the room temperature to the level that you set. Another interesting factor is what is called free heat gain. Having a thermostat in every room enables one to save fuel by utilizing this free heat gain from sources such as sunshine, domestic appliances and people.

# CHAPTER NINE

# ELECTRICS

## IDENTIFYING ELECTRICAL FAULTS IN THE HOME

Arriving home on a cold winter's evening, we expect to be warmly welcomed by bright lights at a touch of a button, an instantaneous hot shower, a comfy chair in a warmed room, a hot drink and a favourite television programme (remotely controlled, of course!). We take all this for granted.

Electricity is not the mystery that most people believe it to be. It does not take a scientist to understand the wiring in a home but it does help to have some knowledge of the basics, to make the best use of it and to maintain uncompromising standards of safety. Electricity is produced at power stations for immediate use. Immediate is the operative word because electrical energy cannot be stored and it does not burn like gas, coal or oil when it produces light, heat or power. A large number of power stations are located around the countryside, to supply different areas, but also to cope with sudden extra demands in wintertime. Engineers then have to switch on additional generators.

Copper and aluminium are the most commonly used conductors of electricity. It also flows readily through water, earth, air and humans! Insulators, most commonly plastic and rubber, resist the flow of electricity. The voltage of electricity in the UK is 240 volts and a minimum size cable is necessary to safely carry this amount. In many countries 110 volts is common and it is safer for human beings but has the disadvantage of needing thicker cables. Everything that uses electricity from a mains supply is connected by a specially designated cable of a particular size. All electrical equipment uses electricity at a particular rate called the wattage. One of the factors governing the size of cable is the amount of power an appliance uses; in other words, the number of watts. An average light bulb is 100 watts and a one-bar electric fire 1000 watts (or 1 kilowatt). If a one-bar electric fire is on for an hour, 1 kilowatt of electricity is consumed. 1 kilowatt hour (kWh) is the standard unit of electrical consumption and our electricity bills are charged at so much per unit. Your current electricity bill will show the exact price per unit, so you can actually work out what any piece of electrical equipment is gong to cost you to use.

Every home has a consumer unit or an

older fuse box and a meter. The Electricity Board's main supply cable safely terminates at their main fuse and meter in your home. Your responsibility is to ensure that the rest of your home is made safe by following the rules laid down by the Institute of Electrical Engineers Wiring Regulations document. Stringent rules are covered by the IEE for everybody's safety. This document should be in every home and everybody should be familiar with its contents. After an installation is completed the Electricity Board will refuse to connect your wiring to theirs if any part of it does not comply with these regulations.

## CIRCUIT BREAKERS

What used to be a 'fuse box' is now a 'consumer unit'. Technology has brought about a doubly-safe consumer unit, fitted with miniature circuit breakers connected to each circuit in the house. These circuit breakers are so hypersensitive that as soon as there is a leakage or a fault in an appliance, the current is instantaneously switched off. From the consumer unit separate circuits are run around the house. Each lighting circuit using a 1mm cable should supply no more than 1200 watts or 12 lights using 100 watt bulbs. Each ring main, or power circuit using a 2.5mm cable should not serve a floor area of more than 100 square metres. Cookers with a load greater than 3000W (3kW) must have their own radial circuit using a 10mm cable connected directly to the consumer unit and a 45-amp fuse protecting them. This applies also to immersion heaters, but the circuit can be run in 2.5mm, two-core and earth cable, protected by a 20-amp fuse. Storage heaters are run separately in 2.5mm two-core and earth cable to their own consumer unit.

Cable or flex in domestic wiring is made up of three wires. The live (or line) wire, colour coded red or brown, carries the electricity to the appliance. The neutral wire, colour coded blue or black, carries the electricity back. And the earth wire, colour coded green or yellow and green, is the safety wire. Every earth wire in every part of the electrical installation is linked to a common earth point at the meter position. In turn this is connected to the earth terminal provided by the Electricity Board, which is also bonded to all metal, water and gas pipes. Together with circuit breakers the most important factor in an electrical installation is earthing.

In the past, most earthing in an electrical installation was linked to the cold water supply pipes, so that earth linkage current passed out along the metal water pipes into the ground in which they were buried. Improvements in technology have brought about a change. Flexible pipes are now being used underground that are not made of metal nor are they electricity conductors. However, all metal pipes in your home – water and gas – must be cross-bonded, that is, connected and linked to the clamp on the service cable sheath and therefore any leakage runs straight to the earth. The earth clamp, installed by the Electricity Board, is a very important safety connection, therefore should never be removed. All pipe work in the home should be connected to the earth terminal in case one of the live conductors (wires) in the house should accidentally touch a pipe at any time.

Nowadays, a new consumer unit will have its own miniature circuit breakers connected to every circuit in the house. In the event of a fault in any circuit, the miniature circuit breaker will trip to the off position, isolating that particular circuit. Open the consumer unit lid to find the faulty circuit by switching on again. If it will not stay in the on position, carry out the following tests to find where the fault is. Each miniature circuit breaker is marked and numbered, so begin by unplugging all appliances on the faulty circuit. This is to ensure that this particular circuit is not overloaded. If the circuit is still faulty the probable cause is a loose wire in a socket outlet or light fitting. Switch

off at the mains and inspect each one. A loose wire touching one of the other wires, other terminals, or perhaps the outer casing, can be the cause of this short circuit.

If a circuit is not working at all, you must unplug everything or switch off lights in that particular circuit. To test which appliance or light is faulty carry out this test. After having unplugged everything or switched off all lights, replace the fuse or switch on the miniature circuit breaker. Switch on appliance or lights one by one until the fuse trips or blows again. Remove the faulty appliance and restore the circuit to live.

Don't ever be tempted to take on an electrical repair job that is beyond your capabilities. Remember, electricity can be lethal! Don't take risks. If in the slightest doubt phone a qualified electrician.

## FUSES

There is a mistaken belief that a fuse will prevent electrocution. However, the main purpose of a fuse is to protect the wiring, not

you! The thinnest wire in the circuit, the fuse, is the safety wire. Without the protection of a fuse, wires could overheat and

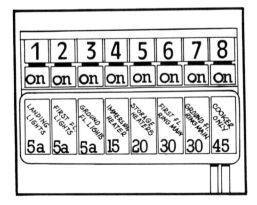

In an emergency you'll need to know exactly which fuse governs which circuit in the consumer unit and what rating the fuse is. Mark each circuit on the lid of the unit after carrying out the following checks. Switch off the power, take out the first fuse or switch off the first circuit breaker, then switch on the power. By trying all the lights in the house, you'll find the ones that don't work — which will be on the circuit without the fuse. Repeat with all circuits. Plug in a table lamp to all sockets to check each ring mains (power). Also check that the fuse ratings are correct.

cause a fire. If too much current flows through a cable or flex it is the fuse wire that melts or breaks, cutting the current immediately. Fuse wires or cartridge fuses have to be of the correct rating. Each circuit in a consumer unit or fuse box is protected by a particular fuse or miniature circuit breaker. By taking out a fuse carrier you find a single- or double-bladed contact at each end. If the fuse wire is present, it has got to be of a certain thickness or amperage. A lighting circuit is governed by a 5-amp fuse, an immersion heater by a 15-amp fuse, storage heaters by a 20-amp fuse, power or ring main circuits by a 30-amp fuse, and a cooker over 12kW, a 45-amp fuse. The fuse carrier will either have a cartridge fuse, just like those in an ordinary plug though of a different size, or a re-wireable fuse which is a thin wire held at each end by a screw in a terminal. Never ever be tempted to use anything other than the correct size of fuse wire or the correct cartridge fuse. Hair grips, paperclips or nails must never be used as an alternative, a fire will certainly be the result. Square-pin plugs have a cartridge fuse meant only for a standard 13-amp plug. Check all your plugs and make sure that any appliance up to 720W is protected by a 3-amp fuse. Appliances rated between from 720 to 3000W should be protected by a 13-amp fuse.

## PLUGS

Cheap plugs should never be used. Plugs marked with the British Standards number BS 1363 are the only ones that you should use in your house. It is the duty of everyone capable of wiring a 13-amp plug to learn how to do it safely. A screw located between the pins holds the cover to the body of the plug. Inside are three terminals and the fuse holder. Strip the outer sheathing of the flex for about 2in (50mm) without damaging the insulation to the separate conductors or wires. Hold the flex at the position of the clamp so that you can cut each of the core wires to length. These should lie without twists in the correct grooves. The green and yellow or green wire is secured to the earth

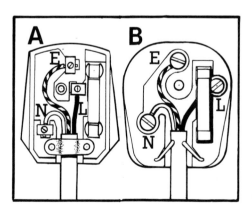

Only buy plugs marked BS 1363 which conform to British Standards. Check all the plugs in use periodically and check that the correctly rated fuse is fitted. An appliance up to 720 watts takes a 3-amp fuse and from 720 to 3000 watts takes a 13-amp fuse. (**A**) is a post-terminal plug, (**B**) is a clamp-terminal plug where the core strands are wound round the studs clockwise. In both plugs check that the outer insulation is held securely by the cord grip and not three core wires.

terminal 'E', which is usually in the centre of the plug. Be sure that the insulation covering of the core wire extends to the terminal. The brown-covered core wire is secured to the live terminal 'L', which is the one connected to the fuse. The blue-covered wire must be connected to the terminal marked 'N' which is the neutral terminal. Double check that all the wires are held securely in the terminals and that no 'whiskers' or stray strands of wire are left unconnected to the terminals to cause problems. Where the cable or flex enters the plug is a clamp which should grip the outer insulating sheath and not three separate wires!

Should an appliance have only two core wires without the green and yellow earth, then that appliance is double insulated, in which case connect to the plug using only the 'live' and 'neutral' terminals. On the market is a cable and wire stripper, an inexpensive tool essential for the ease and safety involved in wiring appliances and the dozens of plugs we seem to have to use each year!

A number of problems can arise in fittings and plugs. Overheating, indicated by scorch marks around the pin holes, can be caused by plugs fitting loosely into connections. Fittings which themselves are loose, cracked or damaged are also a danger. Overloading a socket with two or three adaptors can cause overheating and result in a fire. Carry out a comprehensive check and solve all these problems with new fittings and plug tops.

Never use the smaller, cheaper neon testers for testing whether wires or terminals are live. The neon light hardly shows up, especially in daylight. What is needed is an

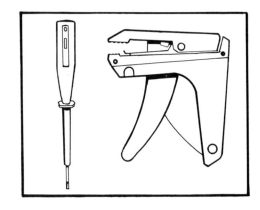

The mains test screwdriver should be used before working on any appliance, even if the power is turned off. It can be used to test mains power cables, sockets, switches, lampholders and circuits. It has an easy to see neon indicator. Other features are the fully-insulated hand grip and shaft and the non-roll protective profile. You should also keep a wire stripper in your toolbox.

electronic 'mains tester'. The best and easiest to use is the type that looks like a chunky screwdriver with the neon indicator located in the insulated handle. Always use one to test whether terminals or wires are live before working on any appliance even though the power may have been turned off. Most of the blade, too, is insulated which makes it doubly safe. Cover the metal cap on the handle with your finger tip and touch the terminal or wire with the tip of the blade. The neon indicator in the handle lights up if the terminal or wire is live.

An inexpensive socket tester can also be a life saver. This cleverly designed tester looks like an ordinary plug but has three neon lights on the face, which indicate the wiring problems in a faulty socket. It can identify the following results:

1   No neutral wire
2   No earth wire
3   Live and earth wires reversed
4   Live and neutral wires reversed

Faults in cables, switches, fuses, circuit breakers and junction boxes can be detected with a voltage sensor. A lightweight pen-sized 'voltstick' discovers where live voltage is in any cable and quickly finds a dangerous break in a cable. It can be used quite safely on cables and flexes with voltages as low as 100 and cables up to 1500 volts. To find cables hidden behind plaster in walls use a specially designed metal detector called a cable and pipe finder. Technology has improved so much that it will not only detect hidden cables in a wall but indicates by light and sound when power cables are live!

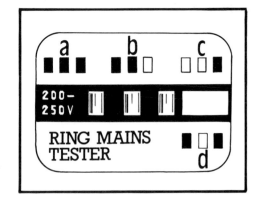

It only takes a few minutes to test every socket in the house with a Ring Mains Tester. The back looks exactly like a plug with three square pins, and is fitted into a socket just as easily. As soon as it is plugged in the three neon lights in the centre light up to indicate an earth fault, that live and neutral are reversed, that a neutral fault is indicated, or that the socket is correctly wired.

## SAFETY FIRST

The use of electrical equipment outdoors need not be the hazard that it was. With the protection of a Residual Current Device plugged into the socket indoors and the appliance plugged into that, any leakage or fault that occurs will, in a split second, cut the flow of electricity. As an extra protection, always wear rubber-soled boots when working with electricity in the garden.

Finally, remember this when dealing with electricity – others, including members of your family, will be using the installation that you have fitted or repaired. Take steps to ensure absolute safety when dealing with electricity and electrical appliances. Faults cannot and should not wait to be rectified.

Remove an appliance or light fitting that is plugged into a socket before you work on it. All connections should be checked a second time before being reconnected and switched on. With the 'safety first' rule in mind, switch off the power at the mains and remove the circuit fuse before carrying out any inspection or repair work on that circuit. Buy the best tools that you can afford for any electrical job and make sure that all the handles are adequately insulated. Finally, if you have to call in a professional electrician check that he is registered with the National Inspection Council for Electrical Installation Contracting (NICEIC).

## INSTALLING A DOORBELL

Another simple and satisfying DIY job is fitting an inexpensive battery-operated doorbell. The kit includes everything that you need to fit the doorbell, except the batteries to power it! Before you start, it is important to make some notes. Stand outside your front door with the door closed and note the best position for the bell push. Take into account that a hole has to be drilled for the bell wire. The bell wire, once through the hole, has to run the shortest distance possible to the bell chime box. Make a note of where that is to be located, so that the bell wire can be effectively hidden.

The box housing the batteries and bell chime can be installed in a convenient position but should not be fitted over a radiator. Most parts of the house can hear the chimes from the entrance hall which is obviously the best place to locate it.

Drill a small diameter hole to suit the bell wire in the wooden frame through which the wire is to pass. If only a narrow part of the frame is exposed then drill as straight as possible. To avoid splitting the door frame when the drill bit comes out the other side, wrap a piece of tape around the drill bit ⅛in (3mm) less than the thickness of

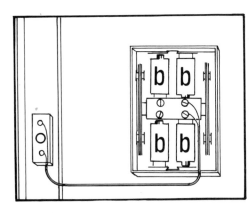

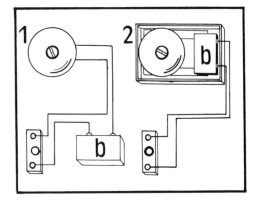

Door chimes are bars hung vertically either side of the batteries which sound different notes when the plunger is activated by pressing the bell push button. When the button is pressed it completes the circuit that supplies power to the two terminals in the bell push and the two in the chimes box. Either wire can go to either terminal, but batteries (**b**) must be inserted correctly, following the manufacturer's instructions. If the battery is separate from the bell, run the bell wire as illustrated (**I**), below.

Separate the twin wires, connect them to the terminals in the bell push and run one to the battery (**b**) and the other to one of the terminals on the bell. The wire to the battery is cut and connected to the second terminal before connecting the other end to the second terminal on the bell. The job is even easier when the battery (illustration 2) is housed in the bell box. The bell wire is connected to both terminals in the bell push and to the battery terminals.

the timber. Drill only a little at a time, with-drawing the drill bit to clear the debris and to cool it. When the tape touches the frame and with only ⅛in (3mm) to go, use this DIY trick to stop the timber splitting. Get some-one to hold a chunky piece of timber very tightly behind the hole position. Drilling through gently will now give a clean hole inside.

Without cutting the copper core wire, trim off the insulating material to be able to fix the two wires to the terminals of the bell push. Check that the screws are tight before locating the bell push over the hole in a level position. Fix it firmly with the two small brass screws supplied.

Take the cover off the bell chime box and hold it in your chosen position to mark the screw holding positions. Nothing looks worse than a lop-sided fitting, so do use a spirit level, and mark the positions on the wall by pushing a pencil through the screw holes in the back of the box. Use a masonry drill bit, as recommended by the manufac-turers, to match the plugs and screws sup-plied. If the box is fitted to timber obviously use a wood drill bit of a smaller size just for a pilot hole.

With the back of the bell chime box screwed in position, the next stage is to pin the bell wire into position using tiny staples. The fine insulated bell wire is only two-core for a battery-operated door bell. It is usually white and can be run unobtrusively under dado rails, up behind architraves and over the tops of door frames. When you arrive at the box, cut the wire to enable sufficient of the outer insulation to be trimmed back to fix the core wires to the terminals. Instructions on the box will tell you exactly how to do this. Also take note from the instructions of the positions of the batteries. Even though it doesn't matter which wire goes to which terminal, it does matter how the batteries are installed. The attractive cover is usually held by integral clips and only needs a push to click it into position.

Simple to fix and simple to operate! Now check outside by pressing the bell push. This action activates an electromag-net, which causes a metal striker to hit the bell or chime. As the metal makes contact with the bell it cuts off power to the magnet, so the striker returns to its original position. This quick make-and-break action is repeated as long as your finger depresses the bell push. A similar action takes place when chimes are used instead of bells, but in this instance when the bell is pushed a spring-loaded plunger inside a solenoid is activated to strike the tube. Lift your finger from the bell push and the spring throws the plunger to the second tube sounding a dif-ferent note. Chimes and bells make a pleas-ant change from the harsh banging of a door knocker, are inexpensive to install and will give years of service.

# CHAPTER TEN

# FIREPLACES

## REPAIRING A CRACKED FIREBACK

An open fire is part of our heritage! It is inviting, provides a focal point and is a real comfort whenever it is lit. However, the radiant heat that it provides is also heating the firebasket and the surrounding firebrick. Firebacks usually come in separate pieces and the intense heat can cause the lower part of the fire back to expand, while the upper part remains static. Four-piece versions are available, having separate side pieces. In order that the fireback can expand without cracking, the separate pieces are slotted together to rest on a noncombustible tape.

New firebacks usually come in two halves separated under the knee. The lower half must be eased in on to the back hearth and swung around to sit comfortably behind the front surround. Between the fireback and the surround, packing is inserted to be compressed as the mix of 4 parts vermiculite to 1 part lime is filled behind the fireback. As the second piece of the fireback is built into position, continue to back-fill with the same mix.

## REPLACING A FIREBACK

It is unlikely that a fireback is so badly cracked that it has to be completely removed and replaced; however, if you are confronted with that problem, it is not difficult to lever out the broken pieces and the rubble behind. Most old firebacks are stamped with a maker's mark or name which solves the problem of deciding what to order as a replacement. If you cannot find any marks, take measurements of the height, width and depth and ask for a replacement which complies with British Standards and has a high knee. The knee is the protruding part of the fireback facing you (and will cause problems if it is too low!)

Before fixing the new fireback in position, offer the lower half into position to check that it sits centrally in the opening. Pull it forward so that the sides sit behind the fire surround. Check also that there's room for the top half to sit comfortably on the lower half. Lift off the top half and begin filling behind the lower half of the fireback. Use a layer of corrugated cardboard between the infill material and the fireback. Use either vermiculite mix or rubble, mixed with 1 part lime, 2 parts sand, as the infill. (Cement used in this mixture would be too strong and cause a great deal of cracking.)

Once it is set and the heat has destroyed the corrugated card an expansion joint has been formed. If vermiculite is used, add 1 part lime mixed with water. A non-inflammable rope or tape is used between each of the pieces to allow for expansion. The top half must on no account overhang the lower half, but should be set back by at least ⅛in (3mm) to prevent its lower edge being subjected to excessive heat. Fill in behind the top half with the same mix and level the infill to the top of the fireback.

With a mix of 4 parts sharp sand to 1 part lime and rubble, fill the space around the top of the fire back. Slope it to about 45° up to meet the chimney opening. There should be a smooth line, with no protrusions, from the back of the knee up to the back of the flue. Allow three or four days' drying-out time before enjoying the comforts of your new fireplace!

## REPAIRING A CRACKED FIREBACK

If the fireback shows signs of cracking, wait until the fireplace has cooled then use a wire brush to clean the area vigorously; this will reveal whether they are superficial or serious. Vacuum all dust and debris before commencing repairs.

It is necessary to undercut any crack

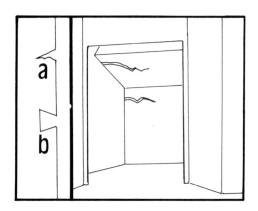

Firebacks often suffer cracking but this is not always serious. Surface cracking (**a**) can be raked out and undercut as illustrated (**b**). This will provide a good key for the fire cement. Always rake out all debris and clean up the dust before dampening the whole area. Never use ordinary cement but a proprietary brand such as Pyruma. It is an easy repair to carry out and should last a long time.

before filling. The use of a bolster chisel and a club hammer is recommended but could result in further cracking if harsh tactics are used. Old firebacks become brittle, so it might be a better plan to use an old screwdriver or file to gently rake out cracks. The raking out process is simply to ensure that the fire cement is pushed in far enough to hold without falling out. Use only fireclay cement, available from all DIY supercentres, for the repair work. Splash the area with plenty of water so that the cracks are thoroughly soaked. Load and press in the fire-clay cement with a trowel or an old knife and point it up as you go along. Be certain that the crack is well filled and dampened before any subsequent filling. This is a very easy and satisfying job and the repair will last for years if correctly carried out. Drying out takes about a day, then you can enjoy an evening in front of a warm fire.

## REPLACING A FIRE SURROUND

In the three decades after the 1920s, period properties, especially Victorian ones, suffered at the hands of 'improvers'. Beautifully moulded dados were ripped off walls, delicately moulded panelled doors were insensitively covered with hardboard and, perhaps worst of all, exquisite Victorian fireplaces were ripped out and dumped. Mostly they were replaced with a small, simple, tiled fire surround and tiled hearth. Fortunately, over the whole country, a reappraisal is taking place and proper restoration is being carried out. An appreciation of classical designs is evident not only in cars, buildings and furniture but also in fireplaces!

The demand has been so great over the past ten years that manufacturers have reproduced authentic designs. New marble fire surrounds made in four pieces can be carried home in the boot of a car. For the enthusiastic DIYer, it will take less than a day to fix the surround in place. Victorian cast-iron surrounds are just as easy to fix but, of course, are heavier to handle.

To make the job of removing the existing fireplace easy, it is necessary to have some knowledge of how it was fitted in the first place. Essentially, the exact internal construction of the opening, throat and gather must be retained when improving and fitting a new, front fire-surround. The illustration shows the lintel or brick arch, which must not be disturbed. The fireback with its protruding knee is an integral part of the design, to overcome potential downdraught problems. Smoke blowing back into a room can be the result of turbulence above the pot, or it may be caused by a fireplace opening that has been changed and enlarged.

Design features, originally intended to ensure the efficient operation and burning of solid fuels in an open fire, became standard. To be effective a flue depended upon certain constructional features being properly built in. For example, the hearth opening was constructed with splayed sides to divert the flow of air from the room into the grate and up the flue. The height of the opening over the fire was 28 to 30in (700 to 750mm) because this height proved to be the most effective. The chamfered lintel above the

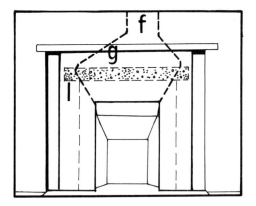

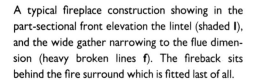

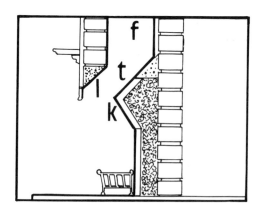

A typical fireplace construction showing in the part-sectional front elevation the lintel (shaded **l**), and the wide gather narrowing to the flue dimension (heavy broken lines **f**). The fireback sits behind the fire surround which is fitted last of all.

The cross-section of a typical fireplace demonstrates clearly the relationship between the component parts. The lintel (**l**) is angled to help the flue gases escape; the narrowing of the throat (**t**) opens up into the flue (**f**). Notice that the knee (**k**) and the lower half of the fireback have a vermiculite mix as back-fill levelled off at the throat. Then the flaunching, a triangular shape, is formed to run smoothly into the gather.

opening was designed at that height so that the air from the room being drawn into the flue would first come into contact with the fire. The now heated air and smoke from the fire was guided through an inverted funnel construction built just above the fireplace into the 9 × 9in (230 × 230mm) flue, as you'll see from the illustration. It is also very important to retain the narrow throat just above the knee of the fireback.

It makes sense to have the chimney swept before carrying out any repairs or improvement works on the fireplace. Clear as much of the furniture as is practicable from the room and roll back the carpet. Use dust sheets and wear a dust mask for your own protection.

The hearth is usually fixed in position after the existing surround has been fitted, so it needs to be levered away first. If you're

working on a solid floor, you'll need to bring the level of the hearth area up to that of the floor. A bag of ready-mix concrete is ideal for this job; mix it following the manufacturer's instructions. Pour it into the uneven hole that is left and level it by simply drawing across the top with a batten. The edges of the existing floor will act as a guide.

If you're working on a suspended wooden floor, the hearth will rest on a concrete infill but the edges of the floor boards and possibly some joists will be exposed. A heavy timber called a trimmer runs parallel with the hearth and is located just underneath the front edge of it. This is supported by two joists at either end and its purpose is to support the intermediate joists which have been cut short. So it is extremely important to examine as many of these surrounding joists as possible for worm or rot. Probably none will be found, nevertheless treat as much of the timber as you can get to with a preservative. Take care not to spill it on to the lath and plaster or plasterboard ceiling below. It will only create another DIY job! Bring the base for the new hearth up to the level of the floor as before.

A fire surround is fixed in position with as few as four fixing points, sometimes even just two. A small piece of metal with a hole in it is already fixed to the back of the fire surround at the top, protruding, so that a fixing can be made through these lugs. Either nails or screws could have been used to secure the fire surround. Sometimes lugs were located at the bottom of the side columns or at the inside position at the base of the column. Tiled hearths and tiled surrounds were actually cast in separate pieces and each section tiled by the manufacturer. Lightweight reinforcing steel bars would have been used in the construction. However, it is possible to break up each piece with a sledge hammer or even a club hammer.

Remove as little plaster as possible to locate and release the fixings. Penetrating oil will release screws and a small wrecking bar is the best tool to lever nails, metal fixings and eventually the surround itself. Use an old mattress or padding on the floor before lowering it – a second pair of hands is useful at this stage.

Repair broken plaster with a DIY tub of one-coat plaster, available at all DIY super-centres. Remember to dampen the area before applying the plaster! While the plaster is drying, you've got time to clear away all the debris and to familiarize yourself with the separate parts of the new fire surround. Check the positions of the lugs, which all fireplaces have for fixing, then find the approximate positions on the wall of the fixing points. Check these areas with a cable and pipe finder to be sure that drilling is safe, but only mark for drilling points when the surround is in the exact central position.

A new wooden surround will have some form of protection from the direct heat of the fire, usually metal inserts. A marble surround has two separate columns, which are fixed first. Usually a mix of cement and rubble is dropped in the base of the columns but the manufacturer's instructions for fixing will be precise. A special two-part cement-adhesive supplied by the manufacturers is used on all marble joints. The horizontal facing is slipped into position and rests on shoulders fixed to the back of the columns. The columns will have cappings or scrolls, the top of which line up with the facing piece. A bed of the cement-adhesive spread over the whole of the top surface will hold the mantelshelf in position. If the mantelshelf is a deep one, with a lot of overhang, it is advisable to chop away a channel of plaster in which to insert the back edge of the mantelshelf. Clean up the channel, especially the edges, and vacuum up the dust and debris. Apply a coat of PVA diluted adhesive to make a bond for the one-coat plaster, which is also used to secure the marble mantelshelf.

If the fire surround is in two pieces, follow the maker's instructions, installing and fixing the inner part first and making a good seal between that and the existing opening. Sometimes the inner part has splayed sides either in cast-iron or a tiled finish, designed to help the flow of air into the grate. It is important that this first piece is fixed properly and very securely. Check whether nuts and bolts are used for fixing cast-iron parts. Whatever the fixing, ensure that no cracks or gaps are left to spoil the efficiency of the burning process. Never use ordinary cement for sealing around the fireplace, only special fire-clay cement. It's as easy to apply as spreading butter on toast! It is readily available in tubs in all DIY super-centres.

Most instructions these days regarding the replacement of a fireback or a fire surround refer to 'expansion joints' and the use of asbestos-substitute rope. If you have to remove old asbestos rope from an expansion joint, the first thing to do is to spray it and soak it with water. Only then is it safe to handle. Previously used as a joint seal, old asbestos rope, once dampened, can be safely raked out, sealed in its own plastic bag and disposed of by your Local Authority.

The size of the brick opening in the chimney breast is calculated to help the fire burn efficiently. A one-piece fire surround is usually not an integral part of this operation. What is essential to keep the fire burning well is a supply of oxygen. As smoke and hot gases rise up the flue they cause a 'draw' at the fire opening, and this suction pulls in a supply of oxygen to keep the fire burning.

If doors and windows are sealed, draught-proofing without some form of added ventilation can impair the efficiency of the fire and cause down draughts and smoke in the room. Ventilation by way of a window vent, under-floor piping or an air brick will solve the problem of an inefficient fire, condensation and its attendant respiratory problems too!

Whatever the period or style of your house or flat, manufacturers have produced a wide variety of fire surrounds in different materials to suit all tastes. A Georgian piece, authentically copied in great detail, is light-weight enough to be carried and fixed by one person. It will have delicately fluted columns, moulded and scrolled facing pieces and a professional overall finish. Look at the back and you'll be surprised to see how simply it is constructed in ordinary pine!

Some manufacturers suggest removing a strip of plaster, so that the fire surround is fixed to the brickwork. Hold the fire surround centrally in position and mark around with a pencil. Cut through the surface plaster skim with a trimming knife ready for removing the plaster with a 2in (50mm) bolster chisel and club hammer. Fix and make good as previously described. If a metal 'trim' or a marble 'slip' is supplied to fill the space between the surround and the fire opening, read the instructions for fixing. Obviously, a noncombustible material must separate the fire and a wooden surround.

## DECORATIONS SPOILED BY BLACK STAINS APPEARING ABOVE A FIREPLACE

Sooty tar stains show up mostly on the chimney breast. The stains can be successfully covered, but until the problem is solved at the source, the effects will continue to appear. For different reasons, these tar stains can occur above a fireplace that is being used *and* above a blocked-up fireplace.

A great deal of kitchen waste such as potato peelings, vegetable offcuts and damp teabags are thrown onto the back of a fire and burned. Fallen branches and logs are cut up and burned as fuel in the belief that they will produce heat and conserve energy. Unfortunately, the gases created by burning wet wood and rubbish cool and condense, more often than not half-way up a chimney flue. The more that is burned, the more condensation soaks into the mortar between the bricks, breaking it up. This allows the dampness to carry the wood-tar deposits and soot through the mortar course to the inside wall. If the chimney pot serving that particular flue does not have a cowl, or some form of protection from penetrating rain, the problem can be compounded.

A fireplace that has been blocked up, with no vent provided, will show similar symptoms. Condensation will be the result and penetrating rain water will add to the problems. As there is no fire burning and no warmth produced, saturation point will be sooner.

One course of action is to burn recommended fuels! A blocked-up fireplace can either be opened up and restored, or a vent installed to ensure a current of air through the chimney flue. Burning wet or green wood will produce enormous amounts of sticky soot deposits in the chimney flue. A build-up of these deposits will not only produce unsightly stains on chimney breasts, but will become a fire hazard. At certain temperatures the build-up of tar will ignite and set fire to the flue. This is unlikely to happen if approved and recommended solid fuels are used.

It is possible to re-line a flue using pumice liners, which come with full DIY instructions. This is a two-man job and should only be tackled by the advanced DIYer!

If no more condensation is being produced, ultimately the flue will dry out, which only leaves the chimney breast problem to be solved. One method of covering it is to batten out and clad with decorative timber panelling. This is covered in Chapter 5. Alternatively use a steam stripper to remove any wallpaper and get back to a sound plaster base. Cut a piece of foil-backed plasterboard exactly to size and use a proprietary adhesive and galvanized nails to fix it to the wall. The aluminium laminated to the back of the plasterboard will prevent residual stains penetrating through the plasterboard. Ordinary plaster or tile adhesive can be used, dotted over the wall to hold the plasterboard in place. Alternatively, lightweight pre-treated battens can be used, drilled, plugged and screwed to the wall, as a framework for the plasterboard. Use a pipe and cable finder (metal detector), so that there's no danger when you drill into the wall.

If the stained area has become very saturated and damp, it is likely that the plaster will be too. If the surface is uneven, chip it out, back to the brickwork and re-plaster with a DIY application of Easi-Plast. Full instructions are on the tub. After the recommended drying time, a simple and effective method of successfully sealing and covering the chimney breast is to paste on a foil-backed wallpaper. This is a laminated lining paper with a backing similar to kitchen foil.

This creates an impervious barrier to damp and stains. Paste it and hang it just like ordinary wallpaper. Having solved the problem of condensation, complete the problem solving by hanging matching wallpaper over the sealed chimney breast or stain and seal the timber cladding to add tone to the room.

# CHAPTER ELEVEN

# BASIC

# SECURITY

# MEASURES

One unfortunate statistic that we are confronted with in all articles on basic home security in magazines is that most ordinary homes are vulnerable and that one in twelve is broken into each year! Everybody needs to play a part in the fight against being a victim of that depressing statistic. Sadly, complacency is often our crime. It is essential that all householders check the most vulnerable parts of the house and take precautions to protect themselves and their homes.

No burglar makes a hole in the walls of your home in order to gain access! The holes are already there, protected only by glass and wood held in place by latches and hinges. Make your own check-list first and then consult your local Crime Prevention Officer (CPO) who is available by appointment at your local Police Station. The CPO will advise on ways to further improve the security of your home. Make your own check-list based on the following points and with it assess all the strong and weak links in your own home.

## CHECK-LIST

1  Is a DIY burglar-alarm system installed?
2  Is the front door fully protected?
3  Are other doors and entrances well protected?
4  Can the porch be fully lit?
5  Do patio doors have a special bolting mechanism?
6  Are all ground floor windows lockable?
7  Are upstairs windows accessible from flat roofs and are they lockable?
8  Louvred windows – is each pane glued in place?

**9** Is the garage door double-locked?

**10** Are garden sheds containing tools fully protected?

**11** Is there a ladder or long pole lying around?

**12** Do hedges provide protection for a break-in?

**13** Can drain pipes afford easy access to windows?

**14** Are skylights kept closed and locked?

**15** Is exterior lighting fitted?

**16** Are keys ever left under stones or flowerpots?

Make your own report based on the checklist before the appointment date with the CPO. Now read through the rest of this chapter before making another list! With your own honest report indicating every vulnerable area, write down suggested methods for safeguarding and protecting them. This guideline and background information will allow you to judge what protection devices are best suited to your home's particular needs.

## BURGLAR ALARMS

Modern technology has brought the burglar alarm system into the DIY market. All DIY supercentres stock alarm systems. Collect a few brochures on different systems so that you can decide more easily on the one most suited to your home. Sophisticated systems connected to a local police station are installed by specialist firms and are expensive. DIY systems are reliable, but remember that even though it might make you feel more secure, it is not a substitute for unopenable doors and windows! The best DIY alarm systems are fairly easy to install. Fully illustrated instructions come with the kit. You have to select carefully the location for the detectors which are connected to a tamper-proof control unit controlled by use of a special key. Do all your own investigation work and familiarize yourself with the information contained in the alarm system's leaflets before the arrival of your CPO. This is the only way that you'll be conversant with his detailed discussion and advice.

## DOORS AND WINDOWS

Fit a peep-hole door-viewer in your front door, a mortise deadlock (BS 3621) and a rimlock preferably the type that has an integral restrainer. This obviates the need for a security chain.

If an ordinary rimlock is fitted and no security chain, use a newly designed door cord. The door cord is actually an immensely strong, flexible wire attached to both sides of the door frame or the brickwork either side. The ⅜in (10mm) diameter wire is covered in bronze plastic, but similar in construction to a ship's hawser. Its strength is not only in the wire itself but the plugs and bolts either side. These are so designed that any extra pressure on the door cord only serves to increase the holding power of the bolts. By pulling at the bolts, the claws inside the plug

The strongest lock for a front door is a mortise deadlock because it becomes an integral part of the door once properly fitted. Fit it in a slot cut into the edge of the door. Always use one protected by a BS No 3621 – it's pick-proof, resists forcing and the bolt is hardened steel.

The rack bolt is an extremely simple device to fit but is powerful and strong as it becomes part of the door once it is let into the edge of the door. A key has a racked end to activate the bolt and these can be fitted to all doors and most wooden windows.

actually open and grip more firmly inside the drilled hole. The door cord is fixed one side and hooked the other and, once in place, allows the door to be opened just 3in (75mm). To allow access simply close the door, unhook the one side and let it fall behind the door.

There are a number of simple bolts available to make all types of windows safe. A sash window lock holds the two meeting rails secure when a bolt is inserted into metal sleeves in each rail. A special key has to be used to unlock the window. A casement window (hinged) can be locked by screwing two separate parts of the lock to the frame and the sash. This can be unlocked only with its own special key. There are many locking devices available to secure a casement stay. The simplest form is a bolt, which

is key operated. A rack-bolt is a simpler form of a mortise-deadlock, in that it becomes an integral part of the door once fitted. It is very strong and can be fitted as extra security to all doors and some windows. If you have metal-framed windows use a lock that keeps the fastener handle in the closed position. A slide moves up and down quite easily and when in the up position the handle is locked. A bolt system called a restricter lock can be fitted to sliding sash windows in metal frames. This restricts the movement of the sliding window itself. It is a DIY locking system, with the lock screwed to the inner sash and the bolt locked into a hole drilled in the outer sash. Sliding patio doors need to have a lock which works from the base of the door. A weakness in older patio door installations made it very simple for the door to be lifted off the track, but now a bolt and locking mechanism needs a special key to release it. Also on the market are locks to fit at the top of patio doors.

The one window that is left open more than any other in most homes is the bathroom window. A rain-water pipe or a soil pipe can usually be found very close to it! Iron downpipes are very strong and fixed very securely to the wall and can be an open invitation to a fleet-footed intruder. But there is on the market a paint that prevents a pipe being used as a means of entry. It is a slippery anti-thief paint for use on iron rain-water pipes which remains slippery, unaffected by the weather making it impossible to grip the pipe.

All other means of entry to an integral garage, through the main door, a side door, a communicating door, outhouses and sheds must also be reviewed and security locks or padlocks fitted. Single storey additions and flat roofs provide an easy means of access to an upstairs window, particularly if there is a ladder or long garden pole available for a would-be intruder. A skylight or dormer window left slightly open for ventilation is also an invitation, especially if the roof is of a shallow pitch construction.

Have you ever left a front-door key under a stone or flowerpot outside the house? A criminal has had far more experience than you in finding suitable hiding places!

When making your check-list, did you walk along the street outside your home? Stand near the front door of your opposite neighbour and check whether high hedges or fences obscure your neighbour's view affording a burglar protection.

## SECURITY LIGHTING

Security lights installed outside your home will make an intruder very wary of approaching it. A simple lighting system can be run from an indoor circuit, but if you're not familiar with installation of lights do seek professional advice. Fittings must be specially designed for exterior use, fully protected and earthed. Some security lights are actually activated when someone approaches, others are switched on and off by dusk and dawn light. If a door viewer, or peep-hole, has been fitted to a front door, it is useless at night if a porch does not have its own light!

## MARKING YOUR PROPERTY

When your local Crime Prevention Officer visits you he will also talk about marking your possessions so that they can be positively identified. There are a number of methods available for marking your property without spoiling the look or value of an article. However, your CPO will confirm that a basic rule for marking property is to select a part of an article where the mark cannot be removed without spoiling the performance or look of the article. If a criminal sees that to remove your marks he has to ruin the article, he'll think twice about stealing it.

An inexpensive set of lettered punches can be used with a hammer on heavier equipment such as lawnmowers. A fine hand-held vibrating marking tool, as used by jewellers, is available in a DIY version. This is simple to use on domestic appliances, videos etc. To mark invisibly any of your property use an ultraviolet pen. This too is available in a DIY supercentre and is used to identify and protect your valuable personal possessions. Mark the articles with the special pen, using your personal post-code, so that you, the rightful owner, can always be identified. These marks will not disfigure or devalue the property but will become visible only when viewed under the ultraviolet light supplied with the kit. All Police Stations are now equipped with ultraviolet scanners so that lost or stolen property can immediately be identified. Included in the kit are security warning stickers advising that the articles are protected by security coding. So that the marks are not affected by constant handling, choose a concealed area. Marks exposed to direct sunlight can fade. Permanence of the marks will vary, depending on the type of surface and the conditions under which the article is kept. The rule is check the markings once a year with the aid of your ultraviolet light and, when necessary, remark.

Everybody needs to play their part in the fight against the growing problem of crime against our homes and property. Make your own check-list, but don't leave it at that. Discuss it in detail with your CPO! Protect your home and property using the best quality devices that you can afford. By doing this you'll sleep more soundly, feel safer in your home and be making a genuine commitment to beat the burglar!

# INDEX

*Index compiled by Peva Keane*